reading this book if you aren't willing to challenge your method of teaching. But if you want to engage your students and have a lot of fun in the process then this is the book for you."

-**Michael Cross**, Assistant Professor of Chemistry, Northern Essex Community College

QUICK STUDENT ENGAGEMENT IDEAS *for* BUSY TEACHERS

Creative Ideas From 1000 Remarkable Faculty & Students

Russ Johnson

Copyright © 2013 by Russ Johnson.

No part of this publication may be reproduced, stored in a retrieval system, or transmitted by any means, electronic, mechanical, photocopying, recording, scanning, or otherwise without prior written permission from the publisher. Requests to the publisher for permission should be directed to: capturetraining@gmail.com

Warning and Disclaimer

Every effort has been made to make this book as complete and as accurate as possible. The author, publisher, and their agents assume no responsibility for errors or omissions. Nor do they assume liability or responsibility to any person or entity with respect to any loss or damages arising from the use of information contained therein.

Paperback ISBN: 978-0-9885925-0-6

Printed in the United States of America

Praise for *Quick Student Engagement Ideas for Busy* [Teachers]

"Russ […] *Engagement Ideas* […] source based on extensive research that addresses the need for college faculty to get on board and make their teaching more active and effective. In his easy-to-read style, Johnson offers dozens of spot-on examples and suggestions using Movement, Materials, Mindfulness, and Media to set a tone for interactivity, discussion, and engagement. Go ahead…it's worth the time!"

-**Sue Landay**, President, Trainer's Warehouse

"As Department Chair for numerous years I read thousands of student evaluations and sat in many classes to conduct faculty teaching evaluations. From this I learned that every teacher, regardless of how highly they were rated, could improve classroom "engagement" activities. Russ provides us all a resource that is loaded with creative engagement ideas and easy to use techniques that are sure to improve our classroom effectiveness and evaluations."

-**Dr. Douglas Miller**, Associate Professor, Hospitality Management, Utah Valley University

"This book has caught the vision of helping educators become designers of learning experiences. It is a must read for every teacher that truly wants to create a significant learning environment in their classroom."

-**Michael C. Finnerty**, President/CEO, NxLevel Education

"Like teachers, professional trainers know the value of engaging an audience so material lands. If you deliver training to corporate audiences, this book will provide you with valuable techniques for achieving that engagement. Take advantage of these ideas to take your training to the next level."

-**Matt Horan**, Global Head of Talent, Mind Gym

"It is liberating to remember that it's not our responsibility to 'cover everything in the textbook'; rather, it's our job to clarify, guide, and help students apply their learning to real-life situations."

-**Debbie Edmunds**, Faculty, College of Nursing, Brigham Young University

"I LOVE this book! As I read it, I kept making notes for ideas I want to try in my classroom. In fact, I started reading it at the beginning of our Thanksgiving break and I was a little sad that I had to wait until Monday to implement some of these ideas. These ideas energized my teaching! I admit, I wasn't sure I would find any new ideas. After 25 years of teaching, I've seen the same ideas repackaged many different ways. This book definitely did not re-use the same ideas. The suggestions in this book would work for students from kindergarten through college!

-**Laura Fenger**, Reading and Language Arts Teacher, Leslie Middle School

"The moment I tried one of these strategies in class I realized that this is a great collection of truly useful ideas. Don't bother

CONTENTS

Introduction – A Poor Teacher ... 1

Chapter 1: Rescuing Ourselves and Our Students from the Deluge ... 7

The Important Balance of Quality and Quantity ... 7
Help! I Think I Might be Boring! ... 8
Why Students Don't Read Their Textbooks
(finally the surprising answer) ... 9
A Performance Plateau Created by Your Favorite Golf Club ... 14
The Inverted Lecture Challenge ... 16

Chapter 2: A New Model of Student Engagement ... 19

You Talkin' to Me? *(The Fickle Student Attention Span)* ... 20
The Enterprising Engagement Model ... 21
The Proof is in the Survey Results ... 23
Engage Me ... 28

Chapter 3: Movement "Less Seat Time" ... 31

Break Those Desk Chains ... 33
Beyond the Classroom ... 46

Chapter 4: Materials "Show-'N'-Tell" ... 61

Too Old for Toys and Games ... 61
Material Matters ... 65
Show Me Your Paper Skills ... 70

Chapter 5: Mindfulness "Flex Your Mind Muscle"   **77**

Deeper Levels of Thought   79
Writing Your Way to Mindfulness   81
Students Take Over   88

Chapter 6: Media "Digital Participation"   **103**

Digital by Design   103
Welcome to My World (Wide Web)   107

Chapter 7: Beginning and Ending With a Bang   **117**

Art of the Start   117
Killer Conclusions   128

Chapter 8: Conclusion   **133**

Appendix: Cheat Sheet *(summary list)*   **137**

"If it's too complicated we won't remember it. If it's too hard we won't use it."
– Russ Johnson

Introduction – A Poor Teacher

My father was a poor teacher. Watching how hard my dad worked and struggled at a sometimes thankless job convinced me that the LAST thing I ever wanted to be was a poor teacher. And now here I am, living the dream as . . . you guessed it, a poor teacher. At least I'm a poor *college* teacher, but—as you well know—that position is certainly not without its own unique set of challenges.

Living in *the interruption age*—where the numerous and varied forms of technology and entertainment seem determined to distract us from any other possible activities—has inevitably made keeping students' attention more difficult, to say nothing of engaging them. Sometimes it seems as if it would be easier to just throw our hands in the air, sing "let's call the whole thing off," and then walk out of the classroom, disgusted over yet another brilliant discourse these students don't get and can only respond to with blank looks or, "is this going to be on the test?" I still see, however, teachers who strive to become better at what they do—who refuse to give up and give in—and they inspire me. They also force me to consider my own performance in the classroom and how I can improve it.

Knowing that the best way to solve a problem is to start at the source, I walked into one of my classes not too long ago and asked, "What makes a sick classroom learning activity?" Blank stare. I mess with them a little. A puzzled, awkward moment of silence later, a student cautiously responded, "What do you mean 'sick'?" I volleyed back, "Well, what does 'sick' mean?" "It depends," she replied. I asked, "Well, 'sick' is good, right? The way I hear you students use the word 'sick' is good. Like, 'Dude, nice ride in the parking lot, "sick"!'" At this point the class looks at me as if I'm radioactive. I must be too old to use the word in that context. I sighed and shifted my vocabulary. "Let me rephrase my question; what makes an awesome, cool, or groovy classroom activity?" making sure to air quote each descriptor and add a touch of "aging-hippy" accent to the last one. My students crack up! They had finally understood the question, and I was once again speaking the mother-tongue of the decrepit and sadly un-cool professor. All was right with the stagnant world again.

That simple act of querying my own students, especially our focus on the definition of "sick," combined with the desire to *be* one of those above-mentioned inspiring teachers only served to further drive home the need for change in my classroom—in most classrooms. Trying to reach students by throwing their own vernacular back at them had emphasized the very base difference in our communication and thought processes—students don't just speak another language, they think in one as well. What I may find engaging and fascinating, they may not and vice versa. The mere existence of those beloved, effective teachers we hear about, and sometimes even see in Hollywood's ever-popular "inspirational educators" genre (think Mr. Holland's Opus, Dead Poet's Society, Freedom Writers, etc.), however, affirms that a middle ground is no myth; effective methods that engage

A Poor Teacher

students and facilitate learning DO exist, they're just not always at the tip of your fingers.

So what does a sick college learning activity look like?

With this question in mind I began to devise a strategy to survey college students and faculty throughout the country. My quest was to explore the inner workings of successful, creative classroom learning activities and principles without having to actually visit any classrooms—I was still a **poor** teacher. I wanted to find out what seemed to work and why; what made students' learning clocks tick and how could we, as faculty, be more involved in the winding mechanism. I also wanted to identify ideas and opportunities that other educators could use in their own classrooms to increase student engagement and create higher levels of learning.

I decided to poll over 1000 faculty members AND college students to discover what teaching and learning methods resonated most with each of them. I wasn't content just to collect tried and true methods and advice from already successful teachers; I wanted to hear what the voices on the other side of the podium had to say as well. Who better to tell us what does and does not work than the recipients of our knowledge? I decided I would also systematically search and sift through interviews, blog posts, and online articles to find innovative yet easy-to-implement learning ideas for a wide variety of settings both in and out of the classroom. If my students could use technology to connect to information and ideas beyond their physical reach, then so could I!

Quick Student Engagement Ideas for Busy Teachers

The numbers from my research told a story, and as I analyzed responses, I began to build a framework that would become a new model for engaging students in the classroom. The data showed that students do want information—and they want it now—but they also want it in relevant and "snack-sized" portions delivered in an engaging manner. After identifying the general principles that most of the responses and research had in common, I came up with a simple but effective way to convey them—strategies that would improve retention, conversion, application, and, most importantly, engagement.

All faculty members can substantially improve their classroom learning environments if they make a conscious choice to apply new ideas and employ the four M's (Movement, Materials, Mindfulness, and Media) of the Enterprising Engagement Model framework set out in this book. By being exposed to these results and strategies, you will discover suggestions and ideas that you can use to tweak or improve your own teaching patterns and routines. I encourage you to openly and honestly ask yourself about the information you will discover within these pages, "What can I incorporate into my own style?"

This book is meant to serve as a tool to help teachers get more out of their students and get more out of themselves. I have included a summarized description of the research findings along with the highlights. I have also presented anecdotes that first demonstrate common challenges and then reveal what others have done not only to conquer these challenges, but to connect with their students while doing so. Furthermore, this book

A Poor Teacher

includes topically appropriate checklists, models, and strategies—all materials that you can use to control your own, custom success plan. From one simple question I opened the door to hundreds of successful learning ideas, activities, and principles.

I hope these ideas will be read, shared, and debated. I encourage you to fill in the blanks for your own brilliant classroom teaching and learning processes. I'm offering you a shortcut through which you can selectively borrow from best practices and start using them immediately. From these "ready-made activities" you can shop for things you like and ignore those that might send you reaching for the bottle (whatever you drink). The pages that follow offer insights into what teachers and students across the country have shared about creative classroom learning activities and experiences, minus a choice phrase or two. My research findings and resulting strategies will also appeal to administrators, parents, trainers and others interested in an engaging learning environment, so if you're not an "official" teacher, you can still easily reap the benefits of my work. I hope I've piqued your interest—you're a little curious now, and eager to turn the next page.

In reality, I'm actually not a poor teacher; I am a rich teacher. I have the greatest job in the world through which I am honored to have the opportunity to share information, influence people, and help build lives. I imagine you must feel the same way too, and I invite you to join me on an intellectual adventure to discover what makes for creative college learning and how you can make it work for you. You might find one or two things here you would expect, but most will surprise you (and some will even shock you, as they are highly contradictory to academic conventions). Get ready for a fun, inspirational, and engaging journey of discovery—exactly what we want our teaching to be! Let the quest for "sickness" begin.

Chapter 1

Rescuing Ourselves and Our Students from the Deluge

The Important Balance of Quality and Quantity

Water gives life, but for it to do so effectively the proper quality and quantity are required. Some bodies of water are abundant yet polluted, like the Ganges in India, and cannot sustain much—if any—life. Others are clean and pure, like a mountain spring, but produce either only a trickle or a vast flood, also lacking the ability to sustain significant life.

Information is like water and the passing on of knowledge too requires proper quality and quantity to reach maximum effectiveness. Most educators don't have a problem with the quality of their content, so the "water quality" is good. It is the distributary overabundance that is most often the issue. An overabundance, or "flood," of information leads to the loss of knowledge down the storm drains of our classrooms.

Sometimes as teachers we think we must always have the answers and must always be right. How wrong that thinking is. It's difficult to discover something new if we already know all the answers. We as teachers dispense information and students can only absorb a limited amount. Too often, however, the flow is fast and furious, causing much of the content to be lost. I call it "informational deluge" or the "fire hose factor;" the stream is unrelenting and powerful, and it is frequently overwhelming. Let's not douse learning enthusiasm, but rather use student engagement to create a wave of learning excitement.

Help! I Think I Might be Boring!

Warning: the following material may be highly offensive to some in the world of academia. To those who practice their profession primarily by lecture, I say "Please don't take offense," but I do encourage you to take a closer look with an open mind. You won't regret it.

Lecture is perhaps the most widely used teaching technique in today's higher education; many universities even incorporate the idea into their titles: Lecturer, Principal Lecturer, Senior Lecturer, Part-Time Lecturer, and Executive-in-Residence Lecturer. Yawn. But does this teaching method, which devours 80 percent of most courses' time, really lead to a *higher* education?

Fine. Lecture is bad; off with its head. Equally important, however, is *why* lecture is "bad." A flood of information overwhelms students and causes retention issues. To put it more bluntly, lectures bore the learning and comprehension abilities right out of students—they contract the often fatal death-by-lecture blues. (Symptoms of the death-by-lecture blues include glazed eyes, slack jaw, lack of participation, secretive playing with electronics, falling asleep, and the "deer in the headlights look" response to being asked "What are your thoughts on what I just said?") During lecture most students are drifting in various stages of boredom. As a business geek I've been known to enjoy hearing the sound of my own voice!

Why Students Don't Read Their Textbooks (finally the surprising answer)

Dr. David A. Wiley—founder of the Open High School of Utah and OpenContent.org, former "Chief Openness Officer" for Flat World Knowledge, and one of *Fast Company*'s One-hundred Most Creative People in Business—recently expounded upon one of the primary failings of lecture. While giving a presentation, Dr. Wiley was questioned as to how to get students to read their textbooks. "I'll tell you exactly why students *don't* read!" Wiley replied. Now I'm thinking, "I've got to hear this!" He continued, "Students don't read their textbooks because teachers tell them what's in them!" He went on to say that students can get up to 70 percent of the information they need simply by coming to class and listening to lecture. Mr. Wiley then continued with a story from one of his own college classes. On the first day of class he told his students he would not lecture in that course, but instead show up each period to happily answer student questions. He then told them, "Read chapter one of your textbook and I'll see you next time." At the next class period Mr. Wiley said, "Good morning. You've read chapter one, what questions can I answer?" At that point there was a quiet, three-minute long, extremely uncomfortable staring contest. No student uttered a word. Mr. Wiley casually said,

> **A Brief History of Lecture**
>
> The noun "lecture" dates from the 14th century, meaning "action of reading, to read." The practice in the medieval university was for the instructor to read from an original source—due to a very limited number of books being in print—to a class of students who took notes on the lecture. Many lecturers were, and still are, accustomed to simply reading their own notes from the lectern for exactly that purpose, regardless of everyone having access to the text(book)s—*which they don't read anyway.*

"All right. Read chapter two and I'll see you next time." During the next class a few students began to raise their hands and ask questions. After about twenty minutes Mr. Wiley excused his students and gave them their, now, routine assignment. The rest of the students caught on and future classes were full of questions, answers, and meaningful discussions instead of lecture-induced blank stares and temporary narcolepsy. There's a lot we can learn from Dr. Wiley.

Rescuing Ourselves and Our Students from the Deluge

What Specifically Is so Wrong With Lecture?

Apparently many teachers are already aware of the dangerously static and unengaging nature of lecture—and the need for innovation. From my research:

"Don't forget that original 'lectures' were the professor reading from the one book as there was only one book back in the Middle Ages. Forms of instruction change!"

"What is never boring is when idiots try to blame others for their failings—'I'm not boring, people aren't engaging properly'."

"Besides teaching college courses, I am also a workshop presenter. If I did not make the workshops relevant as well as interesting, I would not be in business for very long. I try to employ the same principles in my college teaching."

One spirited teacher proclaimed, "Sometimes I use pyrotechnics [as a means of combating boredom]!" While I don't recommend risking arrest (for setting off fireworks within city limits) or setting your classroom on fire, "pyrotechnics" are exactly what more classes need and what more teachers need to be willing to create. Students love bright, sparkly things!

This down-with-lecture mentality isn't exclusive to student victims and perceptive teachers; even Wikipedia, an intendedly objective information source, doesn't "speak" fondly of the lecture method:

> "Though lectures are much criticized as a teaching method, universities have not yet found practical alternative teaching methods for the large majority of their courses. Critics point out that lecturing is mainly a one-way method of communication that does not involve significant audience participation. Therefore, lecturing is often contrasted to active learning...lectures have survived in academia as a quick, cheap and efficient way of introducing large numbers of students to a particular field of study."

Oh Wikipedia, your ability to be both so right and so wrong at the same time is the primary reason we are forced to deny our students use of their favorite paper source. *"Universities have not yet found practical alternative teaching methods for the large majority of their courses."* No alternatives to lecture? There are indeed numerous usable alternatives to lecture—many of which can be used in *every* course—that we will delve into soon enough. But first, there's one more question that needs to be addressed.

Why Do We Continue To Do It, To Lecture?

Why wouldn't we? It's easy, or at least easier. We can practically give lectures in our sleep (and if *we're* virtually sleeping while doing so, it's no wonder our students are nodding off at the same time). Often lecture is a default mode that we fall into. The survey results served to further confirm this explanation with responses such as "I'm getting stuck in lecture mode," or "I just lecture as usual." A few comments were more detailed—and that much more disturbing. One teacher seemed oddly complacent in asserting, "It's either a dry lecture or a lot of work. The problem with assigning loads of work is that I have to mark it. But a dry lecture? I think I can pull that one off." Another defeatedly admitted, "This year I am tired. I am lecturing. I know a lot about my subject and they know zip. I explain and illustrate, they take it in (or not). No more fabulously exciting and hard-to-grade projects with multiple stages. I am tired." Lecture is just easier than doing something new, different, creative, or engaging. However, if we don't want our students "tired" in class, then we need to not give into

> **Periodic Pauses Make for More Learner-Friendly Lectures**
> An interesting study by Ruhl, Hughes, and Schloss (1987) suggests teachers should break periodically from their lectures to allow students two minutes to discuss the content. The researchers compared two styles of teaching: first a forty-five minute lecture without pauses, and second a forty-five minute lecture with three two-minute pauses, roughly every twelve to eighteen minutes, for students to discuss and rework their notes without interaction with the teacher. Students in the second group performed better on both free-recall quizzes and a comprehension test. In fact, the differences were so significant that they would have raised the performance of the experimental students one to two letter grades, perhaps making the difference between passing and failing. So if you still like to lecture from time to time, take a page from Kit-Kat's playbook and give 'em a break.

our own tiredness: we must remember that the work required to create inspiring and creative classroom content is more than worth the return on investment.

Interestingly, some teachers take a rather shocking position, placing the brunt of the boredom blame on students and claiming, "The feeling of being bored is basically a lack of engagement on the part of the person making that comment or expressing that feeling." While the occasional I'm-just-here-so-my-parents-will-keep-paying-for-my-life student may end up in your classroom, determined to learn absolutely NOTHING, this respondent's notion is almost unequivocally WRONG. It *is* the teacher's fault. It's your fault. It's my fault. It's OUR fault. And it's our responsibility to remedy it.

A Performance Plateau Created by Your Favorite Golf Club

Sometimes success stops us, because we're afraid of stepping into something that doesn't work. For many of us, when we find something that works, that is what we continue to do. It works and it's adequate, what more can be required of us? We begin to plateau. One teacher made a very interesting point, that "we do the best teaching in our lives in our first ten years of teaching, when we have the most enthusiasm." Why does our enthusiasm wane? Maybe it does so because the more complacent we become and the inevitably fewer returns we see on our investment, the less we are willing to invest. Our rituals restrict us. Our routines become a trap—a familiarity trap. Our patterns build our prisons. We coast into instructional complacency and we resist change. Mediocrity results from continually walking the same, familiar path. How well-worn is your favorite teaching road?

While recently presenting at a training seminar, I asked the audience, "Who likes to golf?" A number of hands shot up. I turned my attention to one man in particular and asked, "Do you have a favorite club?" He said, "Yes." I asked him how well he would play a round of golf if he only used his favorite club. He admitted with a chuckle, "Not that great." That's what consistently teaching the same way we always have—through lecture—is like; it becomes our "go to" club and our game suffers. We can't afford to remain in the rut of academic "adequacy;" at an institution of *adequate* learning.

A type of apathy or unwillingness to change isn't necessarily at the heart of this problem, however; those are primarily symptoms. Taking a short break from the rigors of writing this book, I traveled to a college in Michigan to deliver a seminar on creative classroom learning. A faculty member explained that as she has so little time to convey all of the necessary information in her courses, it seemed like lecture was the only way to come even close. Can you hear the tick of the curriculum clock? So many of us seem to feel this way, but we must remember, **we don't always have to use the same club**. Too often we just spew our expertise, which can come across to the student as rigid and stale, and hope that maybe some seeds will land on fertile ground—but we don't actually engage in any cultivation; we don't seem to know how. Think about doing more with less—more of them and less of you.

The Inverted Lecture Challenge

If the majority of higher education learning is delivered via 80 percent lecture and 20 percent anything else, then we should reverse and adjust these numbers to 20 percent lecture and 80 percent creative classroom learning activities. Can it be done? Yes it can—even in larger classes! We can be rescued.

To me a good teacher is made up of three parts: one part instructor, one part motivator, and one part entertainer (mix well and serve). It's nearly impossible to be an effective parts one and two if you're a terrible part three. I'm not suggesting you throw on a top hat and tails, but if you can't keep students interested and engaged, then nothing else you do is going to matter. Yesterday a student of mine (name protected) stopped me in the hall and asked, "Russ, can you please teach _____ (name protected) how to be more entertaining while teaching _____ (topic protected in case anyone from my college actually reads my book)!" Shared information is only powerful when absorbed by the receiver on the other end, so we educators must become masters of enterprise who design better, more engaging—yes even more entertaining—learning experiences for our students.

My research has revealed teaching innovations that will take instructors to greater academic heights, regardless of class subject or size, so I am championing change (in my classroom and in yours). Real change starts with a change in thinking. Change the way you think and you will change what happens both in and out of the classroom. Let's create an "innovation agenda" and stop resting on our laurels; let's raise the awareness of best practices and tools for the classroom (that can even help us be more entertaining); and let's eradicate the pain and boredom that lecture causes. Let's create a little fireworks of our own. There are better ways—better tools. Let's roll up our sleeves and see what's in the toolbox.

Final Thoughts

Nobel prize-winner Herbert Simon said, "What information consumes is rather obvious; it consumes the attention of its recipients. Hence, a wealth of information creates a poverty of attention and a need to allocate that attention efficiently among the overabundance of information sources that might consume it." These words hit me like a ton of bricks!

"A wealth of information creates a poverty of attention." At no other time has there been such fierce competition for the student mind. Learners face an ever increasing influx of information from a variety of sources (multiple school courses, television, social media, etc.), but still possess the same, finite amount of attention. Only through new, innovative, exciting, non-lecture (or at least atypical lecture) teaching methods can we effectively leverage our information so that it captures the right amount of the students' attention.

Quick Student Engagement Ideas for Busy Teachers

We have thoroughly sussed out the problems affecting student engagement and touched on the solutions. Now, get ready to discover in depth what is going to help us improve our teaching methods and change the way we teach for good. Better teachers make better students.

Watch closely...here is where I stop lecturing.

Twitter Summary:

Limit lecture—launch innovative delivery methods. Move from academic adequacy to engaged excitement.

Chapter 2

A New Model of Student Engagement

By studying the seemingly elusive concept of student engagement, we gain insights that might otherwise remain hidden: We tend to think we're more creative than we are; we think we're less boring than we are; we give ourselves the benefit of the doubt, which perpetuates mediocrity. Delving into the depths of student engagement robs us of many of our self-assured notions, but in the best way possible.

We realize that, as teachers, we have the critical job of discovering and sharing knowledge, but we have to create a delivery method—an enterprising method of instruction—that guides and facilitates the effectiveness of that sharing. We need to engage students every time we teach and teach students every time we engage them. Engagement is different than passive entertainment. We've already discovered lecture isn't the way to go about this, primarily due to its sheer inundation of information. The truth is, however, too much of anything can wreck the flow of engagement. Why? The human attention span.

You Talkin' to Me? (The Fickle Student Attention Span)

Retention is directly related to attention span; if your students aren't paying attention, they're not learning anything. And students **can** pay attention, but only for certain amounts of time before dozing off, drifting away, or checking out mentally. In the ninth edition of *The Trainer's Pocketbook*, John Townsend asserts, "The brain goes into auto shut-off after only 10 minutes if it is not given something to stimulate it." A study by Hartley and Davies (2004) seems to corroborate Townsend's assertion as it found that immediately after a standard lecture, students remembered 70 percent of information presented in the first ten minutes of the lecture, but only 20 percent of information presented in the last ten minutes. Can you cram all the most important parts of a lecture into the first ten minutes? No . . . or at least not with any explanations or examples (and who needs those, right?) Fortunately, there's a better way.

Attention spans decrease as students become spectators, so introducing activity into lectures can significantly improve a student's informational recall. In their book *Neuromarketing*, Patrick Renvoise and Christophe Morin recommend turning to the "pattern interrupt" method in those moments when a listener's attention commences to falter. Essentially, when a listener becomes used to a speaker's current presentation method—or pattern—the listener's attention begins to fade, leading to a decrease in his or her information-retention abilities. If the speaker wants to maintain the listener's attention, the pattern has to change—or be interrupted. In a classroom situation it is crucial for teachers to switch gears and reengage students just before their attention decreases, whether it be via a new physical, visual, auditory, or mental activity. Breaking up lectures with creative classroom activities acts as a refresh button on student attention spans and brings them back from the brink of unfocused boredom.

So should you switch to an extremely high-pitched voice mid-lecture? Or maybe put on a funny hat? While those options might get you an extra minute or two of attention—though probably not focused on the course material—they won't help you meet your goal in the long run. We have to hold ourselves to a much higher standard than cheap tricks or going for the easy laugh; we have to strive for the kind of enterprising innovation and change necessary to increase the academic vitality in our classrooms (and beyond), to defeat short attention spans by working with and adjusting to them. While this may sound like a herculean task, the solution is actually much simpler than you might think.

The Enterprising Engagement Model

From my research I expected to find complicated models and formulas with which to create exciting new learning activities and combat attention span issues. Considering the "expected" (normal, typical, etc.) in teaching is the problem, I should have known better! When I analyzed the highly effective learning activities submitted by students and teachers alike, what actually surfaced were four simple concepts.

These four fundamental ideas have set a new direction, a new vision, and a new strategy for my classes; they have become the foundation for a new model of student engagement supported by the responses from my research. Together, I call these concepts the Enterprising Engagement Model:

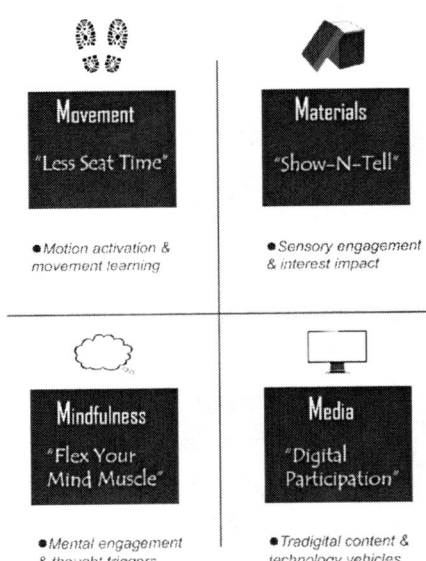

Movement
"Less Seat Time"
Materials
"Snow-'N'-Tell"
Mindfulness
"Flex Your Mind Muscle"
Media
"Digital Participation"

The Enterprising Engagement Model is a platform for innovative teaching. It is a systematic mechanism designed to raise the level of engagement—one in which you are the creative director of your classroom. I constructed this simple, research-based model to serve as a guide for future reference and as an aid to analyze ideas; it is a backdrop for inspired classroom learning and activities. The model is not "THE answer," but a conduit to creating personalized classroom solutions. As long as our learning activities fit into (at least) one of these categories and we keep the attention-grabbing rotation of creative classroom learning activities relatively constant, we will succeed in creating and maintaining student engagement. It's not so much a radical redesign as it is a practical reminder model of simple, yet intuitive principles that contribute to an engaged student.

Sometimes our thought processes become temporarily parked. Whenever I teach the Enterprising Engagement Model findings I have professors come up to me after the seminar and share great ideas that they use in their classrooms. And yet I get the feeling that some of these teachers are saying, "Here is what I do. It works, so I'm ok in the engagement arena." I just want to suggest they be open to new ideas to engage students and not get caught into the familiarity trap of lecture or any other process that can become stale and rigid (even if it *seems* to be working). We need to cultivate an atmosphere of learning excitement through educational agility.

The Proof Is in the Survey Results

You don't have to just take my word on the validity of the Enterprising Engagement Model; the research speaks volumes. Fully 85 percent of the 1000 plus respondents mentioned one or more of the four concepts of the Enterprising Engagement Model—that is a vast majority of both students and teachers. Perhaps even more interesting, however, is what resulted from comparing the faculty responses to the student responses.

When I began noticing the same key words occurring in both student and teacher responses, I decided to compile and compare certain aspects of the data. Of the highly successful creative classroom learning activities offered by teachers, 24 percent of them included at least one of these words: "play," "fun," "humor," "laugh," or "game." Student responses of a similar nature, however, measured at a whopping 40 percent. So, lighten up a little. Play. Have some fun.

A correspondingly surprising pattern emerged with the words "hands-on," "interactive," and "engaging." Only 8 percent of teacher responses contained at least one of these words, compared to student responses equaling three and a half times that amount. While we're desperately searching for ways to engage students, they're practically begging us to do just that; even more, they're telling us how! We just have to put forth the effort; we don't want to end up with a career full of regret like one reflectively honest respondent:

> "Come to think of it, I never made my classroom experience 'fun.' I always tried to pour content into their heads and missed out on the fun stuff. Looking back, I wish I learned or at least thought of much more creative and entertaining learning activities that would have made the information stick."

As I continued reviewing the results, I stumbled upon something unexpected but amazing. For every problem, every complaint, every suggestion a student had mentioned, a teacher (and sometimes several teachers) had provided a solution. In completely unconnected surveys, the two participants in the learning experience had unknowingly worked together to create student engagement. Like many people trying to solve a problem, I had been looking solely for solutions. It wasn't until I saw the responses that I realized a different perspective—the student perspective—of the problem was just as important. They clarified the problem(s) and thus enabled me to more easily ascertain the best teacher solutions.

Meet the typical college student—who has a genuine request:

"I am a student. I am tired (stayed up late). I am hungry (missed breakfast). I can't concentrate (my friends keep texting me). How will you engage me? Tell me a story; a story with characters facing shocking, new or interesting challenges. Then ask me about it, allowing me to be a little grumpy, but encouraging me to continue to participate and reward my efforts. I will cheer up and feel transformed by your class session."

Now meet teachers who rise to the challenge:

"An awesome activity involves all students, captures attention, takes students out of a traditional environment (out of their comfort zone), motivates or inspires action and creates a memory."

"In a great learning environment, the students are all engaged. They might be arguing and sharing perspectives. Many of them would be out of their chairs. The focus would be on a timely topic, and the students would walk away with a memory that will last a long time."

Quick Student Engagement Ideas for Busy Teachers

The interplay doesn't stop there. I invite you to witness actual excerpts of the "conversation" that helped to forge the Enterprising Engagement Model.

Student Suggestions:
"NOT telling students what the course objectives are; rather, asking them what they want or expect from the course."

Activities that are "thought-provoking and hands-on."

Teacher Recommendations:
"Let the students determine the direction of the course with the guidance of the teacher. This way there is so much more buy-in, ownership, and commitment."

"The best activities trigger students to take ownership of the activity."

Student Complaint:
"Quit keeping us chained to our desks."

Teacher Resolution:
"It [an activity] needs to get students up and moving around. Getting students to write on the

> **Mimic Google's Methods**
> One teacher suggested that our classrooms should mimic the "Google 20 Percent Time" rule of thumb. The Google idea is to attract the best and the brightest to Google and allow "smarty-pants" time to let the creative juices flow through innovation. The company's employees are allowed to spend about 20 percent of their time innovating. The teacher's suggestion was to let students determine where 20 percent of their learning (and grade) comes from.

board, move around in groups, present during class time or even take over the class."

Student Requests:
"Get students out of [their] comfort zones, where true learning takes place."

"(Do) something that is out of the ordinary."

Teacher Answers:
Creative classroom learning experiences that include "lots of movement."

Arranging seating "in the round" as much as possible.

"Turning chairs inward creating a circle and having intense discussions and debates."

"Approach[ing] things from a perspective of 'this is wrong . . . why?'"

Student Plea:
"If one would say that the world is your classroom then let's either take the classroom out into the world or bring the world into the classroom."

Teacher Response:
Engage in "any exercise involving real-world, current data—preferably taken live from the Internet or some other source."

Student Assertion:
"The most important part of an activity is the debrief that occurs after, which ties it to the lesson."

Corresponding (as well as more in depth) Teacher Assertion:
"The best classroom activities do two things: first, they propel the students' knowledge and abilities with relation to the course's objectives; second, they open students to larger ways of thinking about themselves and the world."

Despite the fact that there doesn't seem to be a student engagement issue we teachers cannot remedy, many of the surveyed college students said they had never encountered a creative classroom learning experience. So what gives? Often we lack the discipline, creativity, or both to devise such experiences. Hopefully this book so far has helped inspire your disciplinary motivation, and the next several chapters will assist in spurring creativity.

Engage Me

Each of the following four chapters focuses on one of the individual concepts of the Enterprising Engagement

A New Model of Student Engagement

Model. The chapters will not only delve deeply into their respective topics, but they also contain a collection of hundreds of creative and easy-to-use (some easier than others) activities for busy teachers—activities that took many months of sifting, sorting, and evaluating to create and compile. Some activities or ideas that were shared had overlapping conceptual elements, but in most cases there seemed to be a predominant value or principle exhibited (the four "M's"), and that is what has determined in which chapter each activity resides.

May we innovate and inject engagement into our classrooms. This book will shorten the learning curve with hundreds of great ideas. Put "innovative learning" on every meeting agenda, not just during times of crisis which is often the case with innovation. It's about ideas. It's about capturing ideas (in meetings and alone). I love to use lime green paper. I use what I call green notes, small slips of paper (or Post It notes) used to capture ideas. Something comes to mind...write it down on a green note (or any color). The color and size of the paper make it distinguishing and hopefully help it not get buried in our white piles of paper where ideas and information get lost and forgotten. It's about thinking, capturing, trying and then celebrating the results of a newly implemented learning idea.

Author Ken Bain said, "There is no single 'best way' to teach. If we are able to benefit from the insights and practices of outstanding teachers, we must move beyond the stage of 'received knowers,' expecting right answers—tricks of the trade—that we can employ blindly."

Quick Student Engagement Ideas for Busy Teachers

I hope this statement will color how you view the Enterprising Engagement Model and collected creative learning activities. They are not static entities meant to always remain the same and be instituted in the exact same manner; they are tools that can be used to assess and create new activities—ideas that can change as you adapt them to your unique situation.

Let our journey of discovery into the student engagement toolbox begin. We all had teachers that *moved* us. Now, let's look at it—literally.

Twitter Summary:

Surprising research findings compiled into the simple, yet intuitive Enterprising Engagement Model translate to innovative learning results.

Chapter 3

Movement "Less Seat Time"

Much of what happens in our classrooms is content dense and interaction sparse, but when students are asked to participate instead of passively receive information, they stay more focused and are able to learn more. Not only does movement make class more interesting in general, but it actually has a physiological effect on our minds. Studies have shown that when we do something as simple as stand, there is an increased flow of oxygen to the brain, which leads to improved thinking abilities. There is power in movement!

Remember the student who exclaimed "Quit keeping us chained to our desks!" in the previous chapter? He was far from alone in his request for a change of space! He also wasn't alone in his recognition of the need for movement. I received numerous suggestions for movement-based activities from teachers and students, and learned quite a few things about movement myself!

Quick Student Engagement Ideas for Busy Teachers

Adding movement to a class can mean anything from having students choose a side of the room to stand on, to a Spanish teacher illustrating the point of a lesson by stealing his students' shoes; from reading a cold-natured tale outside on a winter's day, to traveling to a ropes course to learn about teamwork. The possibilities for adding movement—spanning from simple to involved—are endless, and the benefits are almost beyond measure.

I like to think of a course's movement options in concentric circles, expanding further and further from the classroom, so let's work our way from the inside out.

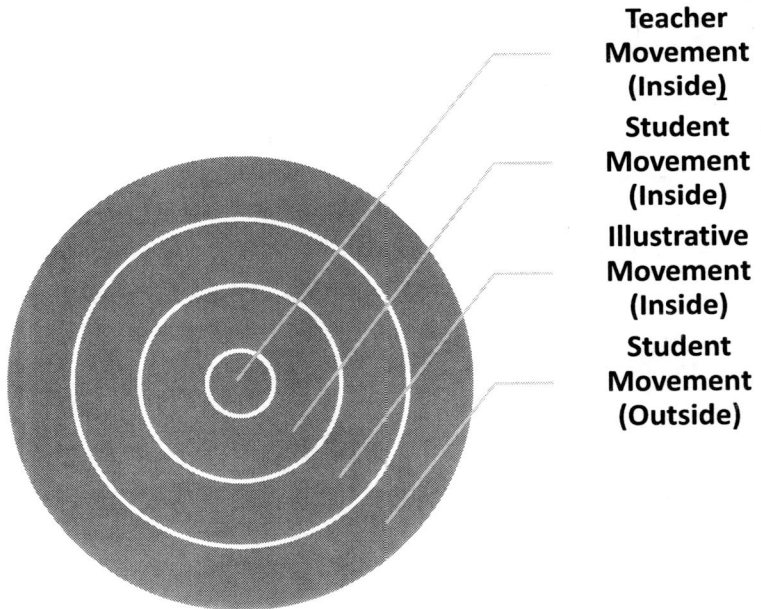

Teacher Movement (Inside)

Student Movement (Inside)

Illustrative Movement (Inside)

Student Movement (Outside)

Movement "Less Seat Time"

Break Those Desk Chains

While I greatly encourage you to explore beyond the boundaries of your classroom, everyday can't be field-trip day or "let's have class outside today" day—in fact, even a majority of days can't be that. Most of the time you need to stick with that meat locker cold or boiler room hot, paper-thin walled, three chairs short of your class size little piece of educational real estate gifted to your course. And that's okay, because you can battle any and all distractions with movement!

Teacher Movement

Sometimes the best place to begin is with yourself. Don't just focus on moving your students; you need to move too! Motion triggers emotion.

Walk the Room
A moving target is harder to hit, right? Not attention-wise. Moving around the room as you teach, instead of hiding behind a podium or holding court from your throne (i.e. that table you sit on) at the front of the room, helps to gain and maintain attention. You might think the pacing can be distracting—and it could be in certain situations—but for the most part physical movement is beneficial. Even in the barest of classrooms, your movement allows student eyes to consistently take in a fresh visual; plus the human eye is drawn to movement, so sometimes you'll catch their attention even if they don't want you to!

Quick Student Engagement Ideas for Busy Teachers

Changing Places

On the other hand, movement doesn't necessarily have to be constant. You can do something as simple as moving yourself from where you normally teach to a different location. One day I came to class and instead of perching myself at the front of the room where every teacher hangs out, I decided to sit on the back row. You know, one of the premium seats way in the back. I can practically hear my students thinking, "What is Russ doing?" Heads are turned. All eyes are on me. My strategy seems to be working. Once all of the students arrived for class and got over the shock of my break in seating protocol, we began a discussion. The students seemed intrigued by the change—despite its minor nature—and tuned in to everything that was being said. Students like seeing their teachers do different.

Talking to One

I learned this tactic from an amazing trainer who has the miraculous ability to keep a large room full of people captivated with his every word and every move. One of his basic strategies was "when you talk to one, you talk to all." Essentially, he picks one person out of the audience and addresses that person in particular as he moves towards him or her. He then picks out another audience member and does the same, continuing this pattern the entire time he is speaking. This method involves the entire audience but each member on an individual level as well, keeping them more invested. He would also take a step closer to his audience in general when he wanted to emphasize a key point.

Movement "Less Seat Time"

Student Movement

While it's definitely good for you to get up and out of your normal space, don't forget that student movement is what sends more O^2 to their brains, so mobilize those students! Sometimes you'll want to ease your students into movement and start with something simple—odds are they're not used to it, unless you're teaching dance. You can then move on to making them move in groups and act as units. And when everyone's comfortable with that, you can pit them against each other and watch the sparks of learning engagement really fly!

Individual Movement
If you think it's best to introduce students to movement with baby steps, then here are a couple ideas that allow students to maintain autonomy but still require them to get out of their seats.

One teacher wastes no time in bringing on the movement: "On the first day of class I conduct a discussion in which I state controversial statements related to course topics and have students either go to the front (agree) or back (disagree) wall. I then ask for a few

> **Out of Their Comfort Zones**
> This same teacher also said something in regards to her movement exercise that I found particularly affecting: *"They actually talked when somewhat removed from the protection of their seats."* This is yet another benefit of movement—it doesn't allow students to hide behind the safety of those desks they both love and loathe being chained to.

35

students from each wall to say why they chose that side." Simple enough, right?

Sometimes movement can be a spontaneous choice, a plan B to keep in your back pocket for when your students refuse to engage: "One thing that's worked for me is having the students stand up and vote on something. Today, for example, I handed out an article from the Chicago Tribune on facial transplants. After they had time to read, I asked who was in favor of this medical miracle. When I got no verbal response—terribly quiet class—I asked them to stand up; 'OK, let's vote with our feet.' They looked at me as if I were crazy. I continued, 'Go ahead. Everyone out of your chairs. It's exhilarating.' Then I motioned to one side of the classroom and said, 'If you're against this new procedure, step to this side of the classroom.' And I motioned to the other side of the room, 'If you think it's a good idea, then you're on this side.' . . . Even with a direct request, students still stood by their desks, feet hardly shuffling. I finally said, 'No one in the middle. You must vote with your feet now.' I then motioned to the folks by the window and asked . . . 'OK, so you think there are problems with this procedure. Why?' . . . After I get a few comments, I asked the students on the other side, 'And what about you? You're for it. Why? What can this medical technique do for people?' I . . . got a few comments." The maestro of movement! Sometimes you just have to persist to get that movement moving.

The "Elevator Pitch" contest brings students to the front of the room to "pitch" their idea. It is usually a 60 second presentation of some kind. It is a short, succinct and

Movement "Less Seat Time"

potentially powerful message conveyed in the most efficient way possible. I have students bring a dollar to contribute to the winner which is determined anonymously by students who vote on 3X5 cards.

Student Interaction/Group Work

If students are accustomed to moving about by themselves, why not have them engage in movement together and reap the benefits of group work as well?

You can start easily enough with one teacher's simple suggestion—an activity that combines the individual with the group: "Take them out of their normal classroom seats—have them sit in a circle, for example, and ask each person to share an insight. Warn them beforehand so they can think of something; maybe have them write it down first, so they don't cop out and just say, 'What Joe said.' (Have each student say his or her name before contributing)."

Another easy and engaging group activity comes from a teacher who makes "puzzle piece pairs where a term is on one piece and the

> **360 Degrees of Movement**
> "I suggest having dry erase boards installed 360 degrees (or as much as possible) around the classroom and create activities that send students to these boards in groups or as a class to work out problems, brainstorm, or write . . . because a teacher can immediately assess the outcome and give feedback. I have used my boards to have students work through Thesis Statement creation, solve a dilemma in a group, demonstrate vocabulary decoding, and so on. Students think better, participate more, and have fun."

definition or example is on a matching piece. Students have to find their matches." Since pretty much every class has its own vocabulary/jargon, this activity could be used for any subject. The next few options require you to divide your class up into groups, so here are a few easy ways to do that. (Letting students choose their groups enables them to stay in their comfort zones and focus more on the people than the assignment. Keeping that in mind, try to put students in different groups for each group activity.) A semi-scientific method for dividing in half is to ask your class to clasp their hands. Normally about half of the class will have their right thumbs on top (of their clasped hands) and the rest of the group will have their left thumbs on top. Try it; it works. You can also divide by birth day (odd or even), birth date (chronology just by the date), age, height, the last time the student went to the movies, etc. You can line-up then count off—students enjoy it. Some teachers like to number off students—let's say one through five—and then put all the ones in a group, all the twos, etc. Want it to be as random as possible? Bring out a hat or bag full of numbered pieces of paper. The number a student draws determines the group he or she is in (plus it adds a bit of movement and materials to the divvying up process). Now that the grouping is done, let's *move* on!

The "Jigsaw Learning Method" is an excellent corporate training strategy that can be successfully incorporated into the classroom. In this technique the teacher divides the class into smaller groups with directions to compile learning points about a specific topic. Each group works on a different topic and the team members become subject matter experts on their particular topic. At the end of a prescribed time the small groups then divide and disperse, forming new groups that consist of one member from each topic. The newly formed groups rotate to all of the topic areas, and each member gets a chance to act as the authority (and spokesperson) when the group reaches his or her topic.

The "Carousel Strategy" is very similar to the Jigsaw Learning Method except that Carousel allows for a greater number of topics. One teacher explains: "Carousel can be used with any subject. As an example, say there is a class of fifty students. Come up with ten different questions, topics, etc. and write each one on a sheet of poster paper (or white board). Divide into groups of five students and have each group go to one of the posters. Ask them to respond to the question (or write what they know about the topic) for a given period of time—a couple of minutes. Then, have all groups rotate clockwise to the next poster, read what was written, and see what can be added. Continue until each group returns to their original poster to see what was added. [You] can cut this short by rotating three or four times and then just have them return to their original poster, but then you'd need to have each group share aloud since not everyone was able to work on every topic/question." These pros use movement to engage their students.

Just as you can take ideas or methods from corporate America, you can take them from almost anywhere else, including the dating world! One student recalls, "In my *English Comp II* class my teacher had the class participate in a 'speed-dating' like learning activity. She passed out questions on a piece of paper, and we each

Quick Student Engagement Ideas for Busy Teachers

spent a few minutes talking about the answer, then we moved on to the next student or 'date.'" Referencing what is apparently a popular idea, a teacher suggested, "You could try the speed-dating one with an application twist—each student has to share a story about how the course content/readings for the day relate to their own life, a personal anecdote, or insight they had. When the game is over, have the class share these, maybe write a few on the board. Helps them see how the course content relates to life."

> **Das Workplace**
>
> "In my social theory class, we do a fun exercise in which students get into groups of four and share their best and their worst jobs. Then we have a class discussion and try to identify the common features of the best and worst jobs. This becomes my introduction to Karl Marx's four-part theory of alienation in the workplace."

Sometimes it's good to have a group activity with a topic everyone can relate to, and one thing most of your students are guaranteed to have had at one point or another is a job: "Depending on your room set-up, put your students in groups of three to five. Tell them that they're going to have the opportunity to 1) complain about a job they hated and 2) talk about a job they loved or—if needed—dream up a work environment they think they would love. . . . You can either have each group do a 'bad' and a 'good' scenario, or assign 'bad' and 'good' to different groups. Let them make lists. 'Hated the way the boss did this...' 'Loved that I was able to do that...' 'Hated that coworkers X and Y could get away with this.' 'Loved that people kept cool desk toys in their cubes.' You get the idea. Make sure to walk around and see what they're coming up with." Tell them about an experience of your own to drive home the lesson.

Debates, Trials, Controversy

One teacher commented that debates can bring greater, more passionate participation; so when you're going for movement, why not go for passion?! Questions? Disagreements. Strong opinions!

A *Social Theory* teacher keeps it simple: "We study four topical issues (climate change, pornography, marijuana consumption, and illegal immigration) and have in-class debates on the issues. The students all help compile arguments and one person per group debates for the team."

In my own *Business Law* class I use an activity I created called "You Be the Jury." The students really enjoy it and it brings a relatively boring subject to life. First, I divide the class in half. One half of the class will play the jury, while the other half will be divided again—into the plaintiff group and the defense group. Next I give a brief background—of a very interesting or controversial issue—to everyone, and the trial teams prepare (on their own time) a common sense argument for or against the case. Then, on a scheduled date, the case (about fifteen minutes) is presented to the jury for their vote. After they have voted, I reveal the actual outcome. The students really eat it up!

Another training based activity that is used during breaks at a conference is to create a "graffiti wall" with either blank posters or rolls of table paper attached to the wall. The idea is to get participants (students) to make contributions by way of written comments on the graffiti wall to keep the discussions alive. Key topics or statements are written at the top of the graffiti wall to encourage further thought.

Here's a creative way to quiz. The teacher's suggestion, "Quiz, Quiz, Trade is where you put test questions on index cards with the answers on the back. Then each student is given a card to quiz someone else in the class. When the other student gives the correct answer, they trade cards and find another student to test." And finally, here's an idea where students interview each other. "Interview classmates about their views on a recent current issue or event; focus on what factors have shaped their views of that event or issue. Each person interprets history a little differently based on his or her background (social, ethnic, regional, etc.)"

Illustrative Movement

If a picture is worth a thousand words, then illustrative movement is worth an entire attention span. Though some of these enterprising ideas could easily fit under one of the student movement categories, there's just something more to them—something visual—that creates maximum effectiveness . . . and entertainment!

"Student" Examples
Nothing makes for better teaching materials than students themselves.

Movement "Less Seat Time"

A fun response included this gem: "In my *History of Creativity* class, my teacher had some boys from the classroom come up to the front of the room to display for us the difference between Romanesque and Gothic arches. He actually had them make a human arch and we all thought they could not do it. It was very interesting, fun, and also educational." (It's enough to make me wish I taught a more visual course, like archaeology or art history!)

In keeping with the idea of using students as building blocks, one teacher reports, "For *Media Law* I frequently have the students participate in a mobile sort of activity with assigned pieces of the litigation process; they then have to arrange themselves into the correct order." An *Accounting* teacher thought along the same lines: "I once turned an accounting class into a human balance sheet. I gave each student a sign that had an account title or balance sheet heading on it. They then had to arrange themselves in the classroom to make a balance sheet." Now, what do you think students will remember more, a teacher lecturing them for an hour telling them all about where things go on a balance sheet or the correct order of the litigation process, or the exercise described above?

While this next example isn't as visual as the previous ones, it's still a great way to utilize students in making an educational point—and it's student approved. A professor was "trying to explain the differences between men's and women's brains and instead of just talking and watching everyone's eyes glaze over, she sent three girls and three boys out into the hall. She had them each come in one by one and explain how to get to the dollar theater.

Quick Student Engagement Ideas for Busy Teachers

All of the boys used directions and street names and all of the girls used landmarks to describe how to get there! It was so funny! When they were outside she had said that—most likely—all the boys would use street names and directions and all the girls landmarks. And they all acted exactly how she said our genders would." Spot on!

All Together Now
The only teaching material that could give a student a run for his or her money is an entire class!

One teacher gave instructions for a whole-class activity used to demonstrate constructive feedback: "Ask for three volunteers. They all leave the classroom. Have the class hide an object (a funny one if possible) in the classroom. One volunteer returns at a time. Instruct the volunteers they are to find a hidden object with direction from fellow students. 1. Bring the first person in. The class will [only] give negative feedback (booing, etc.) when the person is moving away from the hidden object. 2. Bring the second volunteer in. The class provides only positive feedback (cheering, etc.) when the volunteer gets close to the hidden object. 3. The third volunteer is coached with positive and negative feedback when searching for the object. Afterward, debrief with the volunteers and class the experience and differences between the methods of feedback." I know my classes could benefit from an engaging lesson on the importance of constructive feedback.

A student shared an activity in a similar vein that really left an impression on her and her fellow students: "In my *Psychology* class one year, my teacher had a volunteer demonstrate the idea of 'shaping' or 'molding' something into what you want it to be. The volunteer left the room and the class agreed that we would try to get her to draw a smiley face based on our vocal cues. If she drew the picture like she needed to make a smiley face, we cheered. If she started going in the wrong direction, we booed. She eventually figured out we wanted her to draw a smiley face!" Another ringing endorsement of the "show-not-tell" method!

Bring In An Expert

Unfortunately, students won't always know enough in order to be able to create an effective visual lesson (then again, they ARE here to learn), so adding a dash of expertise into your movement can go a long way.

Sometimes you can be the expert, just like this creative language teacher: "In my *Spanish* class the professor was trying to teach possession. As we walked in he took everyone's right shoe and put it on a table in the front. Then, using only Spanish, we had to tell him which shoe was ours. He took everything we said literally. If we said 'his shoe' instead of 'my shoe' he would go and hand it to the 'him' we had referred to. It was a very fun way to learn the correct wording for things."

Other times it's a good idea to bring in some outside help for movement creation: "In a *Hygiene* class we were learning how to best move a patient from a wheelchair into a dental chair. Instead of reading it from a book the teacher had a physical therapist come in and show us. We practiced on each other as well. It gave us the confidence to do it later and it was a fun class as well." Two words. Active participation.

Well, now that we know there's a whole lot of (potential) movement going on in the classroom; let's keep working our way through the circles and step outside for a moment.

Beyond the Classroom

Sometimes the most effective movement-based learning tactic can be a simple change in environment (or even a not so simple one), so when you get the opportunity, take it. And if you don't "get" an opportunity, *make* it!

Field Trips
Field Trips are all about the place—the destination is the star. While most of the other "Beyond the Classroom" activities (obviously) involve getting outside of the classroom, the following prize nothing more than the location.

Sometimes you may only need to step outside for a moment: "Giving students a chance to experience either an actual or simulated activity that focuses on the lesson is valuable. For example, when reading an account of an ascent of Mt. Everest to teach leadership skills, students go outside in the cold temperatures to read the account."

Other times you can step out for a bit longer, but you don't have to go far. I announced to my *Human Relations*

Movement "Less Seat Time"

class the other day, "I've got some exciting news for you: On Friday we are going on a field trip!" The class cheers! "However, there will not be a big yellow bus. You have to provide your own transportation." That Friday we simply walked over to the administration building and had the director of the Human Resource office talk to my class about human resource management issues. Though it may not seem like much, taking my students to that office was much more impactful than having the director come to my classroom.

Occasionally you can go a bit further away and choose a really interesting spot—like a graveyard! Now I've got your attention if you were drifting. I'll bet that would get your students' attention too. One *English* teacher has her students meet her at the town cemetery and then she gives them their assignment: "Write a history of a community, using ONLY the town cemetery as your source of information. Do not write about the cemetery in any fashion; write about the community." And an *English* course isn't the only one that could utilize such a unique setting. A *Geology* course could study the various tombstone materials; a *Medical* teacher could use it as a backdrop for a lecture about death—one that emphasizes the human component as well as the clinical. The location and activity possibilities are limited only by your own creativity. You could take a walking tour of the older part of town for an *Architecture* course or visit the colorful fish at the aquarium to teach your *Art* class about complimentary colors. Even better, why not solicit student ideas? Not only will they have to create connections between particular places and the course, but they'll be all the more invested in the class since they've had a say in its direction!

One of the most popular reasons for field-tripping to an interesting destination seems to be learning about leadership, how to work as a team, or both. One rustic teacher affirms, "I use equine-facilitated education to teach teamwork and leadership skills. This isn't in the classroom; it's at the barn, but the students love it!" Another recollects, "We took our classroom outdoors in the winter in Idaho and had *Business* students go through a ropes course and other initiatives while finalizing product ideas and leadership for student-run companies." Still another teacher mentioned "an introduction course for an MBA program that started with a day in the woods to remind the participants of the basics of communication and team building," while a student gushed, "One of the most effective leadership training college activities I participated in was rappelling to learn confidence in myself and faith in others. It was awesome!" What are the possibilities with your class?

Scavenger Hunts
Want to send the students off on a field trip without you, but still know they'll be busy actually learning? Then try out this old-fashioned favorite. I'll get you started with a couple of ideas, one of which is my own!

One teacher decidedly responded, "I've done a library scavenger hunt; it worked well getting them comfortable in the library." Such a great way to familiarize your students with any campus asset they may never explore on their own. Think they could benefit from a visit to the school's art display? Scavenger hunt. Know that the school's website has some awesome resources? *Online* scavenger hunt. Again, this is an idea that is only limited by your creativity.

For example, I put a bit of a different spin on the scavenger hunt in one of my courses. Students arrive at class one day and I give them a two-page quiz about marketing, branding, pricing, and packaging. I give the class a big grin and say, "Here is your quiz. The answers are at Walmart. I want you to pair up, carpool, complete the quiz, and return to the classroom by 10:45am. Good luck!" And off they run, like little kids at an Easter egg hunt. When they return, we correct the quizzes and have a fun discussion. I've now learned and have to remember to tell them it's not a race (can you picture my running students through Walmart?).

Business Scavenger Hunt

How about a business scavenger hunt? "I teach *English for Business* to visiting Japanese, Korean and Chinese university students. One of the favorite learning activities is a "Business Scavenger Hunt" in downtown Portland. It goes like this: The students form teams of two to three persons each. They are given a scavenger hunt list

Walmart Quiz for Real-world Marketing
- How does the deodorant packaging differ for males and females?
- What's the best ice cream money can buy and how do you determine that?
- What fruits and vegetables are branded?

Quick Student Engagement Ideas for Busy Teachers

with ten questions. They have 60 to 90 minutes to complete the activity and meet at a predetermined location. The team with the most correct answers wins. Prizes are awarded to the winning team members. Questions that are asked for this activity pertain to business ideas like turnover, branding, customer traffic, pricing, etc. For example, I ask them to go into the downtown Starbucks coffee shop and ask what the 'special' of the day is. What does it cost? How many people are inside? What is the average age and dress?"

> **How Many Decibels?**
> Ever want to know just how loud that crowd is? "I had my *Physics 461* class, Introduction to Acoustics, make community noise measurements at BYU football games during the fall. The scenario became fodder for exam and homework questions and classroom discussions and the students had to write a report about their findings. Students commented very favorably about the experience." Who doesn't appreciate a "useful" assignment?

"Another example is to visit both Macy's and Nordstrom, and then compare the 'feeling' inside. How are goods displayed? Does any employee greet them? Which do they prefer? A third example is to go into the tourist information office and ask if they have a brochure written in Japanese (or Korean, or Chinese). Ask for a map of Portland and bring it with you. The instructor can engineer the scavenger hunt list around topics to be covered in class during the period of the course. The sky's the limit as far as creativity is concerned. The students use their English, get to know their new city, and also start picking up business concepts, American style."

Movement "Less Seat Time"
Real World Application

Little is more engaging to students than actually seeing how what they're learning transcends the academic sphere. As one teacher put it, a successful learning activity is "any activity involving getting out of the classroom and putting real world skills to use."

One student remembers learning about just how "dirty" the world around us is: "We went to different parts of the school and collected bacteria with cotton swabs. We cultivated them for two weeks."

This professor gives students a real taste of business: "I teach *Entrepreneurial Finance* and have my students create real companies throughout the semester in small groups, and the rest of the class acts as the angel investors. The group receiving the most votes gets 'funded' and has the opportunity to present to real investors if they would like to actually pursue this idea as a real enterprise, not just a class project."

My *Introduction to Business* class starts a small business every semester. After dividing into teams by function my students launch their business selling everything from t-shirts and hoodies, to hats and concerts. The students take great pride in their business project and learn a little bit about business along the way.

Figure out an activity that will get your students moving and show them how useful what they're learning in your class is. Take *English* students to talk to a hiring manager about the importance of correct grammar, punctuation, etc. on applications, resumes, and cover letters. Have your *Psychology* students sit in on a dog training class and learn a common use for positive motivation. Visit a baking demonstration with your *Chemistry* class and show them that chemical reactions are something we deal with every day, even in the most domestic of activities.

Here is another "real world" assignment suggested by a teacher. "I teach graduate courses, mostly *Government Finance* (Master of Public Accounting program). I assigned my students a project to solve a budget problem in my town. I gave them basic guidance and turned them loose. Their presentations were excellent. No, it was not fun as we would normally think of it. They were cutting a budget. But they learned a great deal and made awesome presentations. They got a taste of political gunpowder."

Community Interaction

And since we're already going out into the "real" world, why not include the community? In these activities students get to escape the four walls of the classroom and reap the added benefits of learning how to work within a community, which they themselves are or will be a part of someday.

Here is an idea that allows students to experience the heterogeneity of the community: "I required each student to attend some kind of event at which most of the people would be different from them. The difference could be race, gender, religion, or anything else, but the point of the exercise was for them to feel 'different.' Before going, they had to write about their expectations of the event and of the people. Afterward, they were required to write about how it really was, how they felt about being different, and how the actual experience compared with their expectations. They were required to turn in their writing, and those who wanted to were asked to tell the class about their experiences. It was an eye-opener for all of us!"

What about involving the local elementary school? "I teach an *Engineering* course where I have students design a semester project that will teach science or engineering concepts to fourth-grade students. At the end of the semester, we bring all of the projects to a local elementary school and allow the fourth-grade students to play with them. This is a great way to help the younger students become excited about engineering and science, and it really gets my students motivated as well."

Use your course's powers for good and for the benefit of a local business like this teacher: "In a *Marketing Research* course I had the students create a proposal and subsequent research tool that was used at a workplace event. The students attended the event, conducted the research, collated the information, and created a final presentation for the board of the event." Students get excited. Businesses benefit.

Real Life Drama

A teacher said, "I have had my *Costume Design* class for four years running design the costumes for a realized play done by our theatre department. So, 10 to 16 students (depending on the year) design a cohesive show. This involves working with the director to evolve a concept, working with each other to make sure every design works as a whole, and working with the costume shop to produce the costumes. Rather than doing paper design project after paper project, this process helps students learn all aspects of the costume designer's work with each student only responsible for their small part."

I found another great idea from the theater department. "In my FYS class we are planning a group piece of guerrilla theater which will take place outside the Student Center during finals week for the amusement of all." Fun!

Service Learning
"Activities that involve service learning that allow students to apply expertise and knowledge they are gaining in the course to real-life community problems are the best learning activities." A very wise teacher. Many schools, including one of my alma maters (which had "Enter to Learn – Go Forth to Serve!" written above its entrance), place a great deal of emphasis on service learning—and they should. Some of the easiest lessons to learn are the ones that make us feel the best about ourselves and our contribution to humanity.

Students seem to respond very well to these types of activities. In one teacher's class they [the students] "decided to take on a service project and collected supplies for Burundian refugees: thirty boxes crammed with household supplies, hundreds of coats. It was amazing! They did it all; we [the faculty] facilitated as needed."

Movement "Less Seat Time"

One student fondly remembers a course in which "we raised money for a teen girl to help her family go on a cruise. This was part of a Make-A-Wish program." Another acknowledges that "compiling ten hours of community service in two different classes was a real reward in the end."

And teachers, like these next three, keep encouraging students to serve:

"I have students in my *Entrepreneur* class participate in the $100 challenge. I put them into teams; they raise the $100 to start up and run a business for four weeks. All proceeds go to www.kiva.org."

"In PBL we host a bead party as a free enterprise project. We sell beads made from recycled paper made into jewelry by women in Uganda who work in the program to provide for their families and give them the ability to live."

A student said, "I went to regularly help disabled children one semester." Another student offered this, "We were required to come up with a service project as a group that would benefit the community. We had to find funds and the means to make it happen. We ended up getting football tickets, game day t-shirts, and free concessions for about 15 patients in the State Hospital. It provided a great opportunity for us to serve in the community while learning how to work in a group effectively to accomplish a goal."

"I teach an *Adapted Physical Education* course in which our students create, design and build an activity station modified for a variety of disabilities. Then we invite 300 kids, ages three to twenty-two, from local school districts to our 'Fantastic Field Day' special event, which is organized and administered by these same students who created the games. This applied learning project encompasses the holistic nature of this particular class. The students tend to go 'above and beyond' the basic expectations of the class because they realize that they are creating an experience of a lifetime for a special child. The desire to provide for others is the culminating, holistic experience of this particular class." These great teachers and students are making a dent in the universe!

I Wanna Go Home

If we move out of the school and business districts, we next will come to the residential areas; I'm talking about where you live. Yes, you the teacher. Have you ever invited your class to your home? I was surprised, shocked really, to discover that a number of teachers do invite students into their homes. I don't know why, as I've done it myself!

Some years ago I wanted to teach my *Human Relations* class about the power of belief. I started with this true story:

> Homes used to require antennae for television reception. One Saturday my alma mater was scheduled to play a televised football game and I needed to quickly install and connect a large

Movement "Less Seat Time"

antenna on the roof of my house. Despite my decided lack of "handy-man"ness, (Bob Vila I was not), I dragged the bulky antenna and my trusty electric drill up to the roof. I then laid on my belly, on the rapidly heating shingles, leaned over the second-story eave (stupid antennae just ALWAYS had to be at the highest and most dangerous point), and attempted to drill through my antenna pipe in order to mount it with a receiving bracket.

I drilled and drilled and drilled, but realized I was not making a dent in the steel pipe. I hadn't used a drill much, but I was certain you could drill through pipe. I had even purchased the appropriate drill bit at the local hardware store. Finally, I was about to give up. No amount of drilling was going to go through that pipe. Then, I looked more closely at my trusty drill and I saw a couple of buttons. I looked even more closely and saw a "forward" and "reverse" switch. I had been trying to drill through a steel pipe in reverse! It doesn't work! I flipped the switch, drilled the hole, attached the antenna, and watched my football game. But the story doesn't end there.

A few years later I decided to save a little money and build my own house. A good friend of mine who knew about the "drill" story said this, "Man, Russ, that would be something if you could go from not knowing how to run a drill to being able to build your own house!"

I visited with another neighbor who built his own house. I said to him you must have to be a contractor to be able to build your own house. He said, "No, you just have to sign your name on the paper stating that YOU are your contractor." You see I didn't believe I could build a house till my neighbor told me I could. I then told my class that they can do anything they want if they only believe. Don't wait till someone tells you that you can build a house or anything else. I'm telling you right now—you can!

I then re-emphasized the power of belief to my class and took them to my new house (which I shamelessly showed off)! I continued, "you can do anything!" Personal stories drive home the learning points in impactful ways.

I'm not the only teacher who has discovered the power of his or her own home. I heard about a teacher who "invites his seminar classes over to his home for a meal, during which everyone discusses the readings," as well as one who came up with a really fascinating idea: Prior to taking a group of students on a foreign learning experience, "we played a game called 'The Culture of . . .'.

The students were invited to freely examine the house of a professor for a limited time (five to ten minutes). They then had to share with classmates what they learned about the culture of that professor. Topics included entertainment, food, shelter/clothing, religion, education, art, music, family, health, etc. It was sure an eye-opener, to see how the students perceived things." I imagine we could all use a lesson in student perception.

Movement "Less Seat Time"

Want Education—Will Travel

Of course, some teachers think that if you're going to go outside the classroom, then might as well go WAY outside. (Which while it won't work for everyone, creates some of the most memorable learning experiences possible).

"I teach an *Experiential* course with another professor on essay writing. We use the outdoors as a venue to stimulate ideas for writing, so we take our students on a three-day cross-country ski tour in the Uinta Mountains and spend time writing in yurts along the way."

Even I've gotten in on the "WAY outside" action. Recently I was involved in putting together a "cruise class" at my community college; we called it the Business Division Cruise to Mexico, a Three-Night Cruised Filled with Business Learning Opportunities. We built up to the cruise with weekly evening sessions in preparation, took a day to drive to and from Los Angeles, and plugged a three-night educational cruise into the middle. I know I speak for myself and all the other participants when I say—AMAZING! Lessons learned on this educational cruise will not soon be forgotten.

You now have all you need to save yourself and your students from a stationary education, so get moving! Next up—material matters.

Twitter Summary:

Strategic movement stimulates the mind and engages the student. Powerful movement based learning beyond the lecterns, desks and classrooms.

Chapter 4

Materials "Show-'N'-Tell"

And the winner is . . . MATERIALS. This is the Enterprising Engagement Model principle that showed up in the highest percentage of responses. Both teachers and students love the idea of bringing something tangible into the classroom other than a textbook—and how could they not? Textbook reading should be saved for homework (unless you're making your *English* class put on *Hamlet*); use class time for fun but relevant activities. And with teachers and students bringing everything from Tinker Toys to marshmallows, M&M's to termites, class is virtually guaranteed to be fun and engaging!

Too Old For Toys and Games

Learning opportunities come in all shapes and sizes. No matter how old we get, we still love toys and games—whether we maybe never outgrew them or just appreciate the nostalgic whimsy.

Quick Student Engagement Ideas for Busy Teachers

You don't necessarily have to raid Toys 'R' Us to engage a bit of the kid in everyone; you can start with something as simple as a ball. One student described an inventive language learning activity: "My *French* teacher wrote a bunch of verbs on a giant ball and when we'd pass it around we'd have to conjugate the word in between our thumbs." A *Math* teacher explained how her examples didn't have to consist of numbers only: "I use my exercise ball to demonstrate the behavior of polynomial functions. I tell them that the floor is the x-axis and the path of the ball is the function. When the ball bounces off the floor, I tell them that's even multiplicity. I then say the ceiling is the x-axis and then throw the ball at the ceiling—it pushes a tile up (ceiling dust then falls on me...students laugh). 'See how the function went through the ceiling? That's crossing the x-axis. That's odd multiplicity!'"

When you're ready to bring in something you'll actually need to visit the toy department for, these two teachers have some great ideas. A *Biology* teacher brought a bag full of animal figurines to class and told the students to "create an evolutionary tree linking all of them together and find evidences showing how they could be related." An *English* teacher has *Introduction to Technical Writing* "students (in groups) build something with Tinker Toys, then write the instruction manual to put it together. The students have a chance to engage their creativity and tie it to a more structured writing task; they also get 'team work' practice." Homerun.

What else can you find with balls and building blocks? Games! And while you can always create your own, there's nothing wrong with getting a little help from

Materials "Show-'N'-Tell"

Milton-Bradley and friends. Several students surveyed excitedly referred to a game called "Star Power" that is used for social experiments. You trade chips for points and the people with the highest points become squares. The next highest are circles and the next are triangles. A certain number of points can move you up or down authoritatively. Then in the next round, the squares get to make the rules. It is a great way to see what people do when given power. Some squares were domineering, while others wanted unity and equality. "A really interesting lesson," said one student. Because I had so many students like this exercise, I bought it. It was a little pricy, but I can't wait to try it out on my *Human Relations* class! Another survey respondent suggested "playing RISK to learn the different theories of international relations." I like to say never underestimate the power of BINGO, especially for *Math* and *Language* courses.

One teacher shared, "For an exam review, I enjoy playing a modified version of 'Who Wants To Be A Millionaire' with my students. I am the host and I present the questions to the students. Correct answers to the questions earn them a prize (usually candy or chocolate). Students have access to the traditional lifelines—I've even had some actually phone a friend outside the class to get an answer. This can be extremely entertaining."

A great activity that is a little more involved, but with greater impact potential is called the "Game of Life." "Students receive an identity that is coded to tip facilitators on how to treat them. As students attempt to get an education or job, the facilitators refuse to serve or push aside those who don't fit the desired criteria. Colors and letters on the name tag are used to designate social classes and prompt certain responses. This activity sets up our reading and conversation of 'little people' as described by Paulo Freire."

Yo-Yo, 500 BC

This one is very good. One day a student came to my *Strategic Innovation* class to give a short presentation. He pulled out a Duncan yo-yo and began to demonstrate as he gave his presentation. The class was mesmerized as he asked, "When do you think the yo-yo was invented?" After a moment of silence a student offered up, "in the 1920's?" Another brave sole suggested the yo-yo was invented in the 1800's. The presenter (Cameron) continued by informing the class that record of the earliest known yo-yo dates back to 500 BC! Yo-yo still going up and down. All eyes are on Cameron and classmates are hanging on his every word. He goes on to explain that in the Philippines the early yo-yo was used as a weapon to apprehend game. It was also used as an early Greek toy, becoming popular in the United States in the 1920's to where it is today. How's that for a long line of innovation?

There is something magical about visual aids. Cameron was able to engage his classmates in a much more powerful way with a yo-yo than without. I have since copied and used Cameron's yo-yo demonstration (and discussion) a number of times.

I like to continue the discussion on innovation by asking the class if they'd be willing to invest grandma's inheritance in a yo-yo business today. "Absolutely not!" they say. I respond right back saying, "What's the matter? People don't buy yo-yo's anymore?" They say no. I say "let's see." I then ask, "Raise your hand if there is a yo-yo in your home." Invariably about half my students raise their hands. Then I gloatingly say, "Oh, people DO still buy yo-yo's!" Then I explain that Yo-Yo Nation will do 1.7 million dollars in sales this year primarily through their website and traveling demonstrations.

Material Matters

Don't think that to find useful materials you have to shell out some of the departmental budget or, even worse, your own cash. Sometimes you don't have to look any further than your own closet.

If you have a bit of the theater in you, why not dress the part? One student fondly remembers when "a *History* teacher presented a very memorable lesson on the1960s by dressing up as a hippie." Another student had a teacher who went a little further: "During a *Chemistry* course, my professor dressed up like a mad scientist for Halloween and showed us the effects of mixing certain chemicals together. Because we were learning about chemical combustion, we were also able to watch what happened when fire was added to the equation." Of course, you could always go the super hero route. Last semester in a *Calculus* class the teacher dashed from the room, saying he was "sick"; when he came back in a few minutes, he was dressed as "Integral Man"—complete with a cape, mask, and t-shirt with an integral symbol. What have you got in your closet?

If playing dress up or morphing into a mathematical super hero isn't really your thing (there are some introverts among us), you can still put a bit of your wardrobe to work by using accessories. This student had a pretty creative teacher: "My *English* teacher came in one day pretending that she had found a purse right before class and began going through it to try to identify the owner. Each item she pulled out generated discussion and then she asked us to write about the owner of the purse." A similar activity using a wallet is described by this teacher: "We've used a wallet sharing exercise to teach about the difference between observation and inference. (The teacher shares his or her wallet as well.) After two minutes to edit out anything the person doesn't want to share, each student examines a wallet and then introduces the person based upon the wallet contents." Aside from being pretty interesting activities, these will probably make you think a lot more carefully about what you carry around with you!

Food Fare
We all know an army marches on its stomach, but can a class learn the same way? We create memories of love, family, and comfort associated with food, so why not lessons?

Let's start out with some breakfast (the best way to begin the day, right?). One culinarily-inclined *Science* teacher "cooked pancakes for the class and related it to *Chemistry*." Several teachers mentioned "potluck review."

Materials "Show-'N'-Tell"

A clever *History* teacher "auctioned off a box of doughnuts in *American Heritage* to demonstrate the laws of supply and demand." I can imagine the first doughnuts went for a fair price with the last few doughnuts commanding more money. One food-based response I really enjoyed reading was this teacher's: "For a 7:30am class, I sent around a sign-up sheet at the beginning of the term (being careful to say that no one was obligated to sign up; this was entirely optional), and everyone signed up for a morning to bring some kind of goodies: oranges, muffins, juice, whatever. It really helped students to know there'd be a little something for them when they got to class, and I think they were more appreciative (and therefore present) since it was their fellow students bringing things in for them, not just me."

> **All Natural and Homemade**
> One student recalls, "[The] most memorable college classroom experience I had was as part of a Food and Nutrition course. One class every student had to bring in a home-baked item made of only all natural products for all the students to sample."

How about introducing some candy into the classroom (and not just on Halloween)? One industrious teacher proclaims, "I love to use food in classroom activities. For *Statistics*, I do an in-class activity where groups of students are given bags of four different types of M&M's candies (I used to use Plain, Peanut, and Peanut Butter, so now I use Dark Chocolate too). Then I have the students do a chi-square test to see if the color distribution is different for the different types of M&M's." Another idea is to play off the names of certain brands.

Quick Student Engagement Ideas for Busy Teachers

You could set up a finals review and reward correct answers with Smarties and Nerds. (You should, however, resist the urge to hand out Airheads and Dum-Dums to those who obviously haven't been studying or paying attention. Their test grades will say it well enough.)

Of course, you don't necessarily have to be able to eat whatever food stuffs you're using. How many different teachers or different classes could find purpose, meaning, and discussion by having class teams build towers with mini-marshmallows and toothpicks? Content for discussion after the tower building contest might include: communication, team building, engineering, planning and development, collaboration, cooperation, strategic planning, competition, leadership, problem solving, creativity, etc. It's a simple yet multi-faceted exercise that engages students.

Chemical Reaction
Science classes are already pretty well-known for a hands-on approach involving lots of materials, but apparently *Chemistry* is where it's at! Even if your own class is far-removed from balancing equations, dissecting frogs, or Newton's theories, everyone has a friend in the science department with access to a few things here and there, right?

One lucky student remembers when "my *Chem 105* teacher was teaching us about molecular weights and gas properties, so he filled two balloons with two different gases; one was helium and the other was sulfur hexafluoride. Helium made his voice go really high (because sound waves travel faster in a lighter medium) whereas the SF6 made his voice almost drop an octave because it was six times heavier than air. It wasn't so much the actual drop but the way he said it. He breathed it in and then ran to the front of the class and shouted, 'Luke, I am your father!'" Imagine teaching a music class a lesson on the different registers of the human voice using that trick.

Some professors prefer the trial-by-fire method of teaching: "My *Honors Chemistry* teacher a few years ago spent a few minutes once each week explaining why certain gasses were particularly flammable or combustible . . . and then lit on fire a balloon filled with whatever gas we had been discussing. Not all classes have the advantage of being able to set things on fire to help illustrate points, but it was certainly effective in that case."

Though it didn't take place in a *Chemistry* class, this student's experience still required some chemical wizardry: "In a *Physics* lab we extracted hydrogen from water and created small hydrogen-propelled rockets and competed against other classmates in determining the optimal mixture to help our rocket be propelled the furthest." Competition is a drug. With engaging lessons like these, it's amazing students become anything BUT science majors!

Living Things
What better teacher than life? I don't mean life as in "life experience" (though that too is an excellent teacher), I mean as in living organisms.

One *Biology* student remembers the teacher who "passed around a plethora of random objects, creatures, substances and [then] we as students were asked to decide if the object was 'dead' or 'alive.' . . . It was a very fun way to be introduced to our section on living organisms (from mold on a potato to scorpions)."

Another *Biology* teacher decided to bring in some pests: "Our *Biology* professor had us place live termites on a piece of paper with a pen circle drawn on it and had us use the scientific method to narrow down the possibilities of why the termites followed the circle around and around the paper. We gave our hypotheses and tested them, and in the end the professor told us the unexpected real reason for the termites' behavior, which was shocking (and funny) enough that we'll never forget it. We learned the scientific method by trying it out." (In case you're wondering, the ink in some pens contains a chemical similar to the pheromone termites use to mark trails.)

If you're an *English* teacher working on passive and active voice or transitive and intransitive verbs, why not bring a (small) furry friend along to demonstrate? Nothing could make your history lesson on Cleopatra more exciting than popping up with an actual "asp" wrapped around your wrist.

Show Me Your Paper Skills

While fun and exotic (to the classroom) materials make for great activities, they aren't the be-all and end-all.

Materials "Show-'N'-Tell"

Sometimes good old paper can be just as effective and engaging; it's all in how you use it.

Many teachers and students commented on the value of finding and bringing discipline-related articles to class. One paper-friendly teacher confided, "I take articles from the *New York Times* (their coverage of labor issues, business, or wealth and poverty works well). I introduce the idea that journalists should mostly be objective, and I have the students find moments of subjectivity in the articles. I'll isolate a few paragraphs, and the students will have to go through each sentence and say whether or not it is a fact, an opinion, or a combination of a fact and an opinion."

In support of the above statement another student said, "Bring in current articles, and apply them to the course concepts." And a teacher said, "I have the students bring articles from the popular press and explain the article with a focus on the science being discussed and the impact on society. We then discuss alternative explanations for what is being asserted and unforeseen consequences, not discussed in the paper. Students write short position

> **Paper Ball Fight**
> Have students write false statements, stereotypes, misconceptions, myths, or excuses regarding your area of discipline. Then give these instructions: "Students, I want you to wad up your paper into a ball. Now for one minute, paper ball fight! Go!" After they're done pelting and being pelted, tell them, "Now pick up a paper ball from the floor and throw it into the trash, because that's where all these excuses/myths belong!"

papers in which they present their positions, explain the arguments on the other side and why the other side's explanation does not change their opinion. These arguments on each side become fodder for class discussion."

Possibly even more popular than articles are index cards—several teachers commented on their various uses of index cards. "I hand out blank index cards and tell students to put 'the good' (something they learned today) on one side, and the 'bad' (something they have a question about—or something they didn't understand) on the back. I use these for discussion the next class period." Another teacher uses "yes" and "no" cards in two different colors. Using a series of questions, the teacher encourages full class participation and makes a game of it. Instead of just raising their hands, the students are more eager to display their "yes" and "no" index cards. I even recently devised an index card-centric activity.

You've Ruined My Weekend
One Friday at the conclusion of my *Personal Selling* class, my eighteen-year old son, Carson (who happened to be in my class—lucky guy), approached me. I had just concluded the class period by giving my students some important, and of course meaningful, homework assignments and my son complained, "Dad you are really piling it on . . . you are expecting a lot out of us!" Over the weekend I kept thinking about my son's statement and decided to put my three-by-five cards to work. On Monday morning I passed out one three-by-five card to each student. First I told the class to write their names at the top of the cards. Then I asked them to list all the

Materials "Show-'N'-Tell"

classes they were taking down the left side of the card with the headings "<u>H</u>" and "<u>T</u>"—Hard and Time—at the top right portion of the card. Next I instructed them to place a number one next to the hardest class in the "H" column, then a two by the next hardest class, etc. I asked them to do the same with regard to time—a one in the "T" column next to the class they spent the most time studying for and so on. My justice was close at hand.

After all the cards were completed, I instructed my students: "Raise your hand if this class is the hardest class you have." Out of twenty-four students, only three hands went up. Then I said, "Raise your hand if this class is the second hardest class you have." A few more hands went up. I went through the same routine with "time." Most students ranked my class somewhere in the middle of both categories. In explanation, I recounted my son's comment, making a rather half-hearted attempt to keep him anonymous, and pointed out that the exercise showed I was not a cold, ruthless professor trying to ruin their weekend plans—that was obviously a title best-suited to some of my peers.

Now, I could have just asked my students to "take out a sheet of paper" and do the same thing, but there is something about an index card that carries more weight, more significance. (I imagine the fact that it is thicker than a sheet of paper makes a difference as well.) I like to think the sturdiness of the cards adds more of permanence to the lesson they are used to teach. It turned into a spirited discussion. I like being a teacher.

Quick Student Engagement Ideas for Busy Teachers

More Paper

Here is something else you can do with a piece of paper. Write different topic headings at the top of each paper (or you can have students come up with the topic). Each student with a paper will respond to the topic (what they know about it). After 60 seconds papers are rotated with students now having a new paper and topic, but the new paper has one student's contribution at the top. More time is allowed for students to read the previous contributions of classmates and then add to them. It's a fun way to "share" learning and force individual thought along the way.

Consumer Goods

Sometimes the best way to show students how a lesson applies to the world outside the classroom is to have them bring items from the outside in—and what better place to get those items than the store? (Just tell your students they're helping to boost the economy.)

One teacher sends her kids to market: "I teach marketing, and for two of my classes, *Packaging and New Products*, I have students bring in items they found in the grocery store to share with the class—good packaging, bad packaging, good new products, bad new products. Both of these exercises are consistently noted in post-class reviews as the most valuable learning they got in the class."

A teacher from an *Operations Management* class tasks her students with bringing in the goods as well: "[I] have students bring in a variety of consumer goods (e.g. water bottle, stapler, flash drive, article of clothing) and have

Materials "Show-'N'-Tell"

class groups identify the various aspects of quality that each of these products possess. They usually are able to identify five to six dimensions of quality. These dimensions of quality identified by the class are then compared to the Dimensions of Quality (Garvin) used within existing *Operations Management* research streams."

I've also heard of *Nutrition* teachers who have students create healthy and not-so-healthy versions of a dish and discuss cost to calorie ratios, and *Economics* professors who assign students to purchase the same (small) items, but from different parts of town. Ever priced batteries from the local convenience store compared to Walmart?

We all are and will continue to be consumers, so lessons utilizing such materials may very well stick for the rest of students' lives.

The above-mentioned categories are but a few in a vast ocean of material opportunities. Why not try taking a fifteen-minute walk in which you list everything you see (that you could feasibly and legally bring into a classroom)? Then take about an hour to figure out a way to use each item in a lesson. You'll be amazed with what you can come up with, and I'd love to hear about it when you do!

Next we're going to think—about thinking. Think about that!

Twitter Summary:

Material elements—introduced by teacher and student—trigger unparalleled attention, interest and learning that lasts.

Chapter 5

Mindfulness "Flex Your Mind Muscle"

We need to show our students how to engage in deeper levels of thought; deeper thought leads to deeper learning. We must encourage and trigger the intellectual labor that will produce greater learning results in our students. We must create and utilize active-thinking opportunities in the classroom. These opportunities will allow students to become more involved not only with our courses, but with their own mental processes as well. We need to both expose students to new ideas and ways of thinking, and help them to realize that their thoughts are important—we need to encourage intellectual autonomy. Think mental gymnastics.

What are the four most important words you ever ask your students? What do you think? No, that's the answer. The four most important words you ever ask are, "What do you think?" It's more than what the teacher thinks.

Students get a lot of that, but what does the student think and why is that important? As we learn to ask better questions we'll tap into a very powerful method for deeper levels of student thought, expression and engagement.

Too often students assume (and we do as well) that teachers "have all the answers" or "are always right." But learning isn't just about having the answers or being "right;" it's more about the journey to those conclusions, the paths of thought that lead us there. Remember the proverb "Give a man a fish and you feed him for a day. Teach a man to fish and you feed him for a lifetime." If you give students answers, they can pass your tests and maybe your course, but if you teach them to think (really think), that's deeper learning!

> **You'll Never Know Unless You Ask**
>
> One teacher regularly asks, "What is the most surprising thing you learned today?" It's a reflective, summary statement. Another teacher "asks students what they think about something they read or heard in the news that relates to the course topic." Asking even simple questions not only engages students, but shows them that you value what they think and have to say—the best inspiration for saying even more!

Put the power of questions to work by increasing the quantity and quality of questions we ask our students (and ourselves). Ask more. Tell less.

The best way to encourage deeper thinking is by using the rhetorical structure that innately requires us to think: the question. Good teachers figure out the right questions. Real learning happens when students come up with their *own* questions. Questions are powerful; they are at the heart of how we engage students. Questions ignite and invite continuous learning, and they open the doors to new learning opportunities. Use provocative questions in teaching to help students flex their mind muscles, to think for themselves, and to engage in deeper levels of thought. I literally cannot count the number of times I've been in the middle of presenting a carefully planned lesson when it veers off in an unexpected direction because a student asks a very interesting question; and that's okay! What better way to encourage student questions and thinking than to treat their thoughts as equally important as your own?

So let's shift those student brains into a higher gear!

Deeper Levels of Thought

It's easy enough to start adding mindfulness to your class with this teacher's simple activity: "Ten minutes before we are due to be done, I ask students if they have questions, and I tell them they can leave as soon as I have answered three questions about today's contents—but not before. It's quite an effective incentive, because even if they think their questions are dumb, they know that all other students will be grateful to them for asking one." The sooner you ask questions, the sooner you can leave; sounds like a pretty good incentive to me!

One student shares how his professor incorporated mindfulness about the coursework: "One of my most effective *Seminar* professors had students bring a one to two page position statement to class answering a question about the session's assigned readings. Half the class would present their position statements and the other half would be responsible for critiquing and responding. The result was that students were clearly responsible for running the class discussion." The more involved students are in the direction of their learning—the more learning happens.

Remember scavenger hunts in an earlier section? Well they're not just for movement! A particularly impressed student remembers a *Writing* teacher who had student groups engage in a "scavenger hunt with our newly assigned peer review groups." As you may expect, it wasn't a typical scavenger hunt. One student was the writer, one the reader, and one the doer. The doer was the only one allowed to actually find the objects and collect them, but he or she was blindfolded. The writer had to write out instructions for the doer to direct him or her to the scavenger hunt items. The reader had to read aloud the instructions exactly as they were written. The student recalls, "This activity was fun and it helped us be more comfortable with our peer review groups." What it also did was make students think very carefully about their communication skills: how they write, how they read, and how they interpret the writing and reading of others.

A *Public Speaking* teacher came up with an interesting assignment that lasts almost the entire semester: "I have them give a speech on a classmate whom they have 'shadowed' all semester. I give them three people the first week of class and then I pick the one that they will speak about at the beginning of December. They have written down things that these people have done or said in class for the semester and it's usually very touching to hear what they say about their classmates (as well as a way for me to see what they have learned from the million speeches they have given in the class)." It's all too easy for students to feel like they're the only ones in or affected by a class, and that is very much not the case in any group outside of school. We don't live and work in bubbles, and this is an excellent activity that ensures students won't learn in one either!

Writing Your Way to Mindfulness

Writing is a way for students to give their thoughts physical form—to "see" their thinking process. It allows for more in-depth thinking than speaking because writing can be edited and re-written—re-worked as more and more ideas crop up or evolve. My research has shown that numerous teachers in all disciplines have realized the value of this type of activity. A "reflection card" or journaling can be a great learning tool.

Why not start class off with writing instead of the traditional (and completely expected) quiz? One pedagogue does just that and more by having students "write out responses to the readings at the start of class (or before class). Sometimes it gets the creative juices flowing. Sometimes you have to force them to read what they wrote, or have them exchange papers and read the neighbor's response. Do the above, but then collect and read selections. Some of them need to hear their ideas in order to gain the self-confidence to speak. They also need to hear you say, 'Now here's a great idea that Antoine has written . . . .'" Mindful and encouraging? I'm definitely going to borrow this idea.

Another fan of the written assignment shared: "I give five-minute 'writing exercises' at the beginning of each class. Students must write for five minutes in response to a question I pose about the reading. I vary the type of question, but I am consistent and serious about these writing exercises. They usually comprise about twenty to twenty-five percent of the final grade. Questions are most often about the author's argument or evidence, but sometimes I lighten it up by asking something like 'What surprised you the most about some of the key points made in this article?'"

And one early-in-class activity—this one by a teacher who has not only created an effective writing activity, but saved himself a bit of grading as well (always a plus): "Having students write group summaries instead of doing a quiz has been a great strategy for me. Not only does it help students remember, process the reading, and get into the day's work, it gives me a wealth of information about what they're reading, how they're reading, and who needs more help."

Wright In the Middle
If immediately jumping into writing when class begins isn't your favorite idea, you can still easily tuck some pensive penning into the middle of class. This teacher not

only has a great suggestion involving response papers, but a unique and interesting way of describing "response" to students: "[I] have students write two-paragraph 'response papers': one paragraph of summary, and one of response . . . [I then explain that] in sports commentary, we have the play-by-play announcer and the color announcer. The play-by-play guy tells you what you already know, what any couch potato looking at the screen already knows [the summary]: who threw the ball and who caught or missed it. The color guy tells you what the play MEANS [the response]: 'And now the Broncos will have a tough time going to the playoffs.' If all you do when you talk about the story is tell what any average person who read it already knows ('and then they all did thus and so'), you're doing the play-by-play. Don't give me [just] the play-by-play. I KNOW what happened. Tell me what it MEANS. Give me the color." Direct hit. I can see it now.

Another example of writing as a response to course content is called free writing. While this can be used in numerous ways, one teacher does the following: "Students free write for five minutes, then they pass their papers to the left (or right) and the next person responds to the first writing by free writing again for five minutes, and then passes it to the left and does the same. I let them pass the papers five times, but it's arbitrary. Students loved it, and we got some really interesting ideas, all of which could have been turned into papers." I don't know about your class, but in my class students are always complaining about how difficult it is to come up with paper topics, so any activity that can help them out gets a thumbs up in my book!

Of course if you'd rather save the writing for last, you can always give the "one-minute paper" a try. About five to ten minutes before the class ends ask your students, "What is the most interesting thing you learned in class today?" or "What is one question you still have?" Give the students a few minutes to muse and then one minute to write. These papers force students to take measure of what they've learned that day (or what they were supposed to) and also allow them to probe the day's lessons even deeper. What you do with those one-minute papers is up to you—some teachers like to respond to them at the beginning of the next course, while others may create more activities from them. Whatever you do, don't let those questions go unanswered!

More Writing
If you're really feeling the writing method, why not devote an entire class period to it? I came across one teacher who suggests, "How about, for a class or two, instead of trying to get them to talk, you have them write? Whatever the subject of that day's discussion is, turn it into one or a couple of writing prompts, and have them spend substantial time writing. Some of the smarter, more (intellectually, if not physically) engaged students might be willing to provide good answers when their peers can't see what they're writing. Then you might be able to use the written responses to get things going in a discussion (but it will require you to call on people, especially those who did well in the writing exercise)."

Mindfulness "Flex Your Mind Muscle"

Another way to spend the last ten minutes is to come up with a "top ten" list. This activity is simply a method of review. In our final minutes come up with a top ten list of things you recall from our discussion today. Then, time permitting, have partners share and compare their top ten list. This is an easy way to review at the end of the hour if you have time.

Ask your students to define a great customer experience. What does it look, feel and sound like? Have students create a list of tangible, observable components of a great customer service experience and see where the discussion takes you.

Whenever you're allowed to have a say in a situation, you're more invested in it, right? Students are the same way. If you let them have a say in what they're learning, or at least in what they're doing in class on a certain day, they'll be more mentally involved. It requires much less thinking to just sit in class and have someone teach "at" you than to assist with or create that teaching.

Sometimes you just have to give students a choice. In my own classes I often walk in and ask, "What do you want to do today?" After we get beyond the inevitable "Nothing, let's do nothing today," I throw out some ideas. They pick or suggest the direction and then are excited to move forward, thinking it was their idea. One happy student remembers her *Evaluation Methodology* course. . . . We had to choose criteria, then evaluate according to them for various brands of chocolate chip cookies, which were then provided for the class! Fun." Circling back to me, I like to give my students a finals week choice: Basically students can choose a much longer take-home final exam or a typical in-class final exam. As you've probably guessed, they always opt for the take-home final—even though it will take them three times as long to complete as the in-class version! They never seem to complain; after all, it was *their* choice.

The next step up from letting students make choices about the class is having them create and plan parts of the course. You can student-up a trivia game with "Fish Bowl Mania. Students write questions on note cards. Put them in a big container. Call on a student to draw a note card from the bowl. Then the student answers or calls on another student (or team) to answer the question. Of course, you can have them write questions solely for you as well. The trick is to stack the bowl with a couple of fun note cards, both clueless and hard high level questions."

Or you can basically have your students tell you what parts of a lesson you need to go over most, like this teacher: "Today I asked them to get into groups and skim the reading homework and come up with their own questions, which worked wonders. I told them I would collect the questions and post the best on the CMS tonight to answer. They seemed actually excited to see what questions I would post."

Student Written Quizzes
I was surprised at how many responses I got that synced up with a teacher who suggested that "students write quizzes and exams." Another teacher divulged, "I divided students up into groups, and then had them write a test of five multiple choice questions about anything we've

covered all semester. They actually wrote some pretty good questions. Then, they traded with another group and took the other group's test. They then traded back and graded the other group. We tallied the points, and it became very competitive." And this next teacher shows me that my final exam "choice" can be taken much further: "I had played with lots of ideas about the final exam, and I couldn't decide on one that 'felt right.' So I opened it up to the class, and asked them to write exam proposals, with justifications for why they thought their exam would be good, given the line we've been walking between writing skills and literature skills." What students wouldn't love the opportunity to write their own evaluatory materials?

But why even stop there? Put students into groups, give them a portion of the lesson, and have them teach it to the rest of the class. Think about how you never *really* know something until you've had to teach it to someone else. (Just don't forget a Q&A session at the end of each lesson—one you can help out with if needed.) It's about students teaching students.

Real-World Applications
As I've previously mentioned, nothing catches student attention more than connecting course lessons to the world outside the classroom. And since getting (and keeping) their attention is half the battle—the engagement half—what better focus to enable mindfulness?

First let's look at some great in-class activities:

Hot or controversial issues can help jolt student thought and feedback. These can be used to "get students to formulate solutions and evaluate responses to solutions. Example: Nobody is happy paying sales taxes. Would you abolish taxes? How will you make up the money lost if sales taxes are abolished?" Another teacher had a unique follow-up to this question and would inquire "if they eliminate sales tax what new tax would they impose, and on what?" Everybody has an opinion, so use that as a jumping off point for more critical thinking.

> **Character on Trial**
>
> A rather litigious teacher suggested, "Put a character on trial: put the main character of a novel on trial, and divide the class into prosecution and defense, and let them dig up evidence from the text to use in court (as well as acting as other characters to be witnesses, etc)." This great idea could also work well for a history course, a law course, or just about any course with larger than life characters in it (whether they're fictional or not).

Students Take Over

A number of responses from my research talked about the value of debates. "I used a debate-like exercise last year that worked really well. Students wrote out a very informal, one-page response to a contentious argument we were dealing with that week. The next day, I had them get into groups of 4 to 6 and share their response papers with the rest of the group. I expected that there

Mindfulness "Flex Your Mind Muscle"

would be some conflicting responses to the reading, and there were. At the end of the group and class discussions, I gave the students about 15 to 20 minutes for in-class writing. I had them play devil's advocate to their own initial response, and write an opposing argument on the back of their initial response paper. They were essentially debating themselves."

Just as debates and trials were great vehicles for movement, they are for mindfulness as well. One innovative teacher shared, "I had students pretend to give testimony at a regulatory hearing on regulating advertising directed at young children. There were many sides to the debate, not just pro and con. For example, manufacturers of cereal had different perspectives than advertising agencies. Similarly, among the opponents, parents had different views than dentists."

Another submitted, "Give them a list of opposing adjectives that might describe the values of a culture, such as: Take time for the customer vs. Be efficient. Loyalty vs. Personal career goals. Do your own work vs. Work as a team. Competition vs. Cooperation, etc. Have students individually choose the 'best' from each pair, then discuss in small or large groups . . . maybe force the group to come to agreement on each (which will spark debate). Have them generate examples of actual behaviors in the workplace that would demonstrate each value. Wrap up with a discussion that none of the values are 'better' but are simply 'different' values."

Some teachers cater to the student interest in the almighty dollar: "I like dividing my class into groups, assigning each a different income, and asking them to devise an annual family budget. This teaches students about how income determines quality of life." A family budget isn't the only budget students will have to contend with either as all businesses, companies, departments, etc. have budgets to follow—and don't forget about state and federal budgets. There's virtually no course you can't create some sort of budget activity for.

Cultural Cues

Others teachers enjoy exploring cultural differences, like the teacher who has students complete a "cultural quiz, trying to match stereotypic statements to different cultures." Imagine the interesting post-quiz discussion about where the stereotypes may have come from, how accurate they are, and how accurate they may or may not have been in the past. You could even bring this type of activity into the academic setting, focusing on the stereotypes of different majors, different professors, etc.

Here is another cultural exercise sure to ruffle some feathers. "The Best Color Eyes." I start by asking a show of hands of those who have brown eyes. Then blue. Then green. "Are there any other colors that I didn't cover?" I ask. Then I pick a color, usually green eyes. If you have green eyes you are very special. We take a quiz. Then I have everyone except green eyes exchange their papers. Green eyes can correct your own paper—because you can be trusted. We do some other things in class, then five minutes before it's time to dismiss my students I say, "Ok, green eyes you may leave. Everyone else please remain seated." It's so unfair!

One student remembered a mindful lesson that was a bit of a shock: "A teacher in an *English* class presented a document for us to examine, not telling us what it was. It sounded like an order to process something, or get rid of something; only afterwards did we find out it was a letter from one Nazi official to another, talking about the Jews and other Holocaust victims. It helped me understand how language can be used in any number of ways, and that there is no one description for anything." If you're ever at a loss as how to help students relate to a lesson, don't underestimate the power of linking ideas to the past.

The Theory of a Firm

One *Economics* teacher decided to get as real as possible by teaching a lesson directly involving the students, their school, and their education: "In entry-level *Economics*, we learn the theory of the firm. A firm consists of (loosely speaking) people coming together to turn raw materials into value-added products, in order to sell them at a profit. So, in that context, here's how an exchange in the classroom goes: Me: 'Let's think about this school as a firm. Who are the owners?' Them: 'The taxpayers, the regents, whatever . . .' Me: 'What is the product?' Them: 'Huh? Uhmmm . . . education?' Me: 'No. Let's try again. Who is the customer?' Them: 'US!' Me: 'No. Let's try again. What is the raw material?' Them: 'Uhmmm . . . duuhhh . . .' Me: 'You are the raw material. Now, what is the end product?' They usually are staring at me with really blank looks by this point, so I spell it out for them. The students are the raw material. The production process involves educating them and spitting them out as finished product, worth much more in the workforce than they would have been without an education. The customers are their future employers (or society at large, if you prefer) who pay a premium for the high quality product that is their educated little selves. The students bear a part of the cost of production, but they are not the customers. They also earn the life-long profits from their education." I've used this exercise several times with great success.

More Real-World Examples

And here's one more example of hitting students with an education-themed, real-world example: "In my *History* class we learned about the rule of law, the principles that make laws generally accepted and constitutional. The next class after learning about it we had a quiz. The quiz was extremely difficult and nobody did well. Afterwards the students voiced many complaints. The quiz had violated all the principles of the rule of law. It was a demonstration of how people react when the rule of law is violated. Everyone received full credit for that quiz afterwards. I thought it was cool that we not only learned the principles of the rule of law, but we also got to see how it could apply today."

Real-world applicable activities in the class are indeed handy tools, but they are still somewhat limited. Real-world applicable *homework* assignments are most effective as well, and they allow students to engage themselves in opportunities a classroom setting limits.

Sometimes these deep-thinking homework assignments can last almost the full term. In a communication class a teacher assigned students to "think of one difficult person they have interacted with who causes tension or conflict." The assignment was to take one insight from the basic *Communication* course and do one thing differently in the next encounter with this person. The teacher had them submit a brief report on the result. The assignment was due in four to eight weeks to give students ample time to plan and reflect. Another teacher recommended "Set[ting] up an assignment whereby the students have to keep a scrapbook on a particular issue or candidate and hand it in at the end of the term. That will get them reading. They will then analyze the material."

Other times mindfulness-inspiring activities may only take a few days: "I invite my students to live lives of perfect integrity for three days, and then write short essays on what they have learned. I do the same with kindness. AND: I ask them to think of someone they have offended or hurt, and then ask forgiveness of that person. Then, they write an essay on what they have learned."

Self-Reflection
The only type of assignment that could possibly hit closer to home than a "real-world" applicable one is a "self-applicable" one. A lesson that affects a student as part of a group can be interesting, but one that affects a student as an individual can be *fascinating*.

Some teachers take aim at students' physical selves: "I teach a course in *Health Promotion*. I have each student complete a self-assessment of his or her health status and then have everyone make recommendations for health improvement related to diet, exercise, life style changes, and socialization. They get to self-reflect and do some 'teaching' with each other as sample clients."

How Much Money Would It Take?
Another option is to encourage students to look inward. One teacher shared this: "When we discuss ethics and values I ask the students to write down how much money it would take to get them to do certain things (such as kill a cat with your bare hands, spit on a picture of your mother, pull out all your teeth, etc.). We then compare answers and show the tremendous diversity of answers in the class. It always generates a ton of discussion (and laughter)."

Another ethics-based activity could involve asking students to pick which super hero or super villain they would be if they could. Then have them list *all* the traits of their chosen heroes/villains—not just the traits they admire or envy. From there you can go in many directions. You can focus on whether the non-desirable traits outweigh the desirable ones (or vice versa). You can see if students still feel the same after looking at ALL the traits instead of just the ones they like. (For example, a student may like Superman's strength, flying abilities, and x-ray vision, but may not like the required Clark Kent alter ego—especially his job at the newspaper!) While this activity starts off as light and fun, it can turn into a very deep exploration of self.

I've taken to encouraging students to better themselves. In recent years I have started having all of my classes read one outside book, usually in the area of self-improvement. Every student has four or five hours a semester to read a book for self-development (that I have approved—you wouldn't believe what some students try to label as a self-improvement book!). No you can't count your science book! Near the end of the semester I have each student give a brief oral report to the class, allowing all the students to hear a few key points from many books. Students also turn in a one-page typed paper, complete with the play-by-play and the color. Another teacher has each student bring a book and throw it in a pile in the middle of the room. Students then pick a book from the pile!

The "response paper" approach is unique and will be remembered. One teacher had almost the exact same suggestion. "Have students write two-paragraph 'response papers': one paragraph of summary, and one of response. They don't take much time to grade. I resisted this idea for a long time, but it works."

Brief Writing Assignments

Here is a great idea I used in my *Human Relations* class when talking about the Johari Window. "In my *Communications* class I have the students get out half sheets of paper and write their names at the top. Then students pass their papers around the room in an organized fashion. Every student is to write one observable thing about the person whose name is on the paper. They continue to pass the papers and add more comments until everyone has his or her own paper back. Students will come up with things like quiet, friendly, open, loud, smart, and many others. This paper helps students see how other people see them. This is a great way to talk about the Johari Window." At the end the original person gets their paper back with some eye-opening insights about them (some flattering and some not). One girl said out loud, "They think I'm stuck up, but I am friendly." I hope she got the message that she sends to others.

In Small Groups
This suggestion from my research involves both elements of "movement" and "material," but I use it here to illustrate the benefits that can come as a result of the movement. The teacher says, "Have students bring with them to class a one-paragraph or one-page response to a reading, theory, what-have-you. Get into groups of five or six (best if you determine the groups, so they don't get into groups with people who already think like them), and share the responses with their group members. Each person will write a short response to his or her fellow group members' assignment, so that each student, at the end of the exercise, will have five or six different reactions to his or her initial response. The person then uses these reactions to write a devil's advocate position to his or her initial response."

Funnies, Interesting and Funny
Another teacher said, "We often try participatory activities like doing a content analysis of the newspaper funny papers (Sunday edition)." A teacher simply said I want you to discuss things like, "How to... ...get fired from a job ...break up with a significant other ...design/decorate your dorm/apartment ...bar hop." Those ideas ought to invoke some interesting discussions.

Mindfulness "Flex Your Mind Muscle"

"The Earth is 1.5 x 10^11 meters away from the sun. Determine the mass of the sun." Everyone looks massively puzzled at first, says the teacher because they're convinced they don't have sufficient information to solve the problem. He goes on to say, "I love watching their faces when they figure out how to do it." Somebody's going to have to help me out here! This one is in the wrong discipline for me.

I do a brainstorming exercise with teams coming up with new flavors and new uses for microwave popcorn. They come up with fun and wacky ideas. They get excited about sharing their ideas. It also creates a sense of team excitement. Students are amazed at how many ideas they were able to come up with in a short period of time.

You Can Negotiate Anything
This will get students thinking. We are talking about negotiation in my *Personal Selling* class. I say anything can be negotiated right? Are you interested in negotiating your next exam? Their eyes light up. They say no exam. I say in exchange for what? And I can't be bought. Whatever you offer has to be related to learning the content of this class. I instruct them to decide what they want and what they have to offer and then come get me when they are ready to negotiate. It usually takes them 20 minutes or so to decide what exactly they do want (usually an early final, or take home exam) and what they have to offer. I want them to come up with things like additional assignments they will do in order to get a take-home exam. It's a great exercise that then enables us to discuss "what happened." I ask them what happened in the room while I was out. Was there true

collaboration as a class or was there some compromise? It is an effective communication exercise.

The Power of Stories

Stories will help engage your students in deeper levels of thought. Get personal. Tell your own personal stories. I have been doing this throughout this book.

Some teachers are reluctant to do this. You have many "teaching moments" that can be delivered with conviction through your own personal stories.

Use real-life and industry stories and examples to emphasize key points. I have told a story about UPS dozens of times relating to the power of information. I start by telling my students I found myself behind a UPS truck the other day. As I was waiting I asked myself this question, "Is he going to turn right or is he going to turn left?" The average driver has a fairly even mix of right hand and left hand turns. Do you think that is true for UPS?

UPS asked themselves a similar question. Their question, "Which is more efficient? Right hand turns or left hand turns?" What do you think the answer to that question is? Students quickly respond, "Right hand turns are more efficient!"

Some years ago UPS realized right hand turns were more efficient than left turns. They re-charted and re-routed their drivers so as to make as many right hand turns as possible. One year after implementation UPS saved 3.1 million gallons of fuel (and vehicle wear, etc.). Isn't it amazing, I tell my students, how a little information can have such far-reaching effects?

Some of my other favorite stories include: Smith Corona typewriters (innovation or lack thereof), Netflix (market response), Ebay (evolving revenue streams) and others.

Many of my survey responses from students said please tell me how what we're learning is relevant and how it relates to the real world. There are lots of real world stories and examples you can weave into your learning.

Fabulous Final Five Minutes
I mentioned earlier ideas for the final ten minutes. I want to propose a Fabulous Final Five Minutes strategy. Rather than fade into the sunset what can you do to capture and utilize those precious final five minutes? If you can build some kind of routine and then stick to it you'll be amazed at how productive those final five minutes can be. It might be a structured method to review and summarize the day's content. It may involve student pairs engaging in a final summary discussion. It may be things we talked about earlier such as the most interesting thing learned today. You may consider a final reminder of things that need to be done in preparation for the next class period. Finally, pique their interest with a mention of what they can look forward to next time!

Less = More
One of the best things about activities that inspire mindfulness is that they don't always have to be super involved. In fact, sometimes students can get the most out of the smallest assignments.

Quick Student Engagement Ideas for Busy Teachers

Short

One "small" assignment aficionado challenges his students by telling them, "You work for an ad agency that has been given the job of developing a public-service ad campaign to alert the public about research" on a particular topic. He then asks things like: What is the slogan? What is the most essential thing you want the public to know? Finally, he has the class "come up with a bumper sticker that tells everyone the basic meaning of the campaign" in the shortest, catchiest way. It takes a lot of thought and creativity to shrink an idea to bumper sticker size. Many bumper stickers, however, are still longer than the next suggestion.

Even Shorter

In a very popular and apocryphal tale, Ernest Hemingway was once challenged to write a story in only six words. His supposed response, "For Sale: baby shoes, never worn," won him the challenge. Why not offer your students a similar task? Maybe have them write about "My College Life so Far" or "Who I am." For a *History* course you could have students write a distinguished figure's six word biography, or for a *Physics* course you could force your students to get creatively concise with famous theories. I discovered this idea on the internet, and I highly recommend using the web to compile excellent examples to show your students. I came across a collection of six-word stories by Iraq-Afghan vets describing their experiences; it was amazing and inspiring. This is short and students love short.

Mindfulness "Flex Your Mind Muscle"

But maybe six words is five too many! One teacher proposed the following single-word based activity: "Each person (of a pair) can say only one word at a time to convey a message to the other in the pair. It really makes him think, because not only does he have to think of what his end goal is, but he also has to listen to his partner very carefully in order to teach the right message." I don't have any suggestions for a "no words" activity (aside from playing charades or Pictionary), but that doesn't mean they're not out there!

Always remember that you are never limited to just one "type" of mindful activity. One teacher who is all about winning combinations writes a "semi-provocative position statement on the board, one related to a central point of scholarly debate on the topic" and then asks students to write for several minutes about whether they agree or disagree and why. Next, students discuss their positions with partners and then it expands to a full-class debate, with half the class taking each side. The teacher added, "EVERY point I would have made in lecture came up, usually with reasonable support."

"Students who usually sat silently jumped in, and light bulbs went off several times as points I had been trying to make all semester finally clicked!" It's all about getting students to engage in deeper levels of thought, so feel free to use every tool you can.

Moving on. I've been waiting for technology to settle down a little bit :). Next stop—technology and the World Wide Web.

Twitter Summary:

Encourage intellectual depth and autonomy by engaging student minds with profound questions and thought-provoking activities.

Chapter 6

Media "Digital Participation"

Regardless of how any of us may feel about technology, there's no avoiding it. But we shouldn't *avoid* it; we should embrace it. The more technology advances, the more opportunities it allows us in our own classrooms and beyond. We can do things we never could before and connect with students in new and exciting ways. You could even argue it's academically irresponsible to *not* use these technological advantages!

Digital by Design

Before jumping into using technology, why not allow for a little discussion first? Here is an anecdote involving a great way to introduce the concept of how technology affects our lives: "After reading a brief excerpt detailing a young child's first experience with an electric light bulb in the 1870s, I tossed out a question to the students about what kind of technological innovations they would point to if given the opportunity to explain to succeeding generations about how much has changed in their own lifetime. I figured I would get one or two comments about iPhones and move on after a couple of minutes. About fifteen to twenty minutes later we had a list on the board detailing everything from digital music and high-definition televisions to portable DVD players to wireless Internet. It was fun to see their faces light up as they thought of something else to add to the list. In the future I'll need to actually plan for this discussion and budget the class time accordingly."

While many people may automatically associate media with technology (and inevitably the *latest* technology), let us not forget that media has been around a lot longer than the internet or cell phones. There are movies, documentaries, and mini-series out for just about every subject—and they only require a DVD and a screen (Maybe you remember when it was a VCR, or even a laser disc!). And what about the old, faithful CD player (which of course has evolved from the record and tape players)? Hollywood has yet to make a movie out of every single Shakespearean play, but *Literature* students

> **Technology Rules!**
> One technologically savvy teacher finds multiple ways to digitally encourage participation: "I have begun putting my reading lists on Google Docs and published it as a web page because so many of my readings are links. Nearly every week I assign a blog, a podcast, some website or other, and often a YouTube or Vimeo video. . . ." He also mentions that "Academic blogs are where a lot of the conversation in our disciplines is occurring. Of course you should introduce your students to this resource."

can still listen to a recording of *The Merry Wives of Windsor* put on by the Royal Shakespeare Company. I knew an *American History* teacher who loved nothing more than to include the soundtrack of the era he was currently teaching. You can still do all these sorts of things now, and more often than not you'll use the all-inclusive internet (or at least items in file formats), but this just goes to show that utilizing media as a creative engagement tool is not a new idea; it has, however, always been a good one. Music to my ears!

Even the Phones Come Smart
Let's start out with a little piece of technology you yourself most likely have and, I guarantee, all your students do—a cell phone. Now, don't think that everyone has jumped on the cell phone bandwagon; if you still don't like them in your class at all, you're not alone. One teacher gleefully admitted, "I . . . show the clip of the professor throwing the kid's cell phone—that's a classic!" A particularly tickled student remembers what one of her professors said on the topic of phones in class: "A professor of mine told me this, 'I am allergic to cell phones; if I see one I will pull a hammer out of my desk and my hammer will have a conversation with your cell phone. Most likely it will be one-sided.'" I've personally considered getting a hold of an old, broken cell phone, telling a class I took it off a disrespectful student, and destroying it in front of them as a warning; they never have to know the phone didn't work to begin with. But in all honesty, vilifying cell phones isn't the most productive route to take.

Quick Student Engagement Ideas for Busy Teachers

Several teachers I surveyed make use of the numerous apps out there: "If you have a 'smart phone,' there's an attendance app that you can download class lists into and then it will randomly pick student names for you to call on." (Let students accuse you of "always picking on me" now!) Another teacher likes to try out polling apps: "By using cell phone polling technology, I am able to gather real-time input from all students, allowing them to see clearly how their perspectives fit in the context of their peers." That sounds a lot better than raising hands and tallying votes on the whiteboard with that dry-erase marker that's two words away from invisible. It only takes a few minutes to open up the app store and type "teaching" into the search bar. You never know what useful tool you'll discover.

Text Me With a Question
Some brave teachers even let students have their phone numbers! (I don't think I'm willing to go that far yet.) This *Chemistry* teacher, however, ended up with a really interesting story to tell: "At the start of class I put my phone number on the board and said, 'Text me sometime with a chemistry question.' A chemistry student texted me asking about her sister's wedding dress. The dress had a tag that indicated that it contained chemicals that are known to the state of California to cause health problems. She wanted to know how much concern they should have about wearing a garment with this tag. I explained that the chemical that it was talking about was probably formaldehyde which is excreted from new plastic material. Most of us know it in diluted quantities as that new car or new house smell. I further went on to explain that getting married was probably more

hazardous than wearing the wedding dress, so in comparison the chemicals should be a minor concern." Hilarious! Texting: allowing you and your students to connect with each other, course appropriate material, and real-world situations. (Plus, who doesn't love weddings . . . and formaldehyde?)

Though if you'd still like to keep a bit of distance between yourself and your students, take a page from this teacher's playbook: "I have decided to embrace the use of cell phones to keep in touch with my students. I have joined Twitter, created a group for my students to follow, and invited all my students to receive and send tweets, via cell phone." See? Student media contact without the total lack of privacy.

Welcome to My World (Wide Web)

And speaking of Twitter, one of the most popular, useful, and rapidly growing group of educational tools consists of that which can be found on the World Wide Web.

Here is an example using Twitter. "I'm using Twitter in a couple of classes to help students connect to professionals and groups who are active on Twitter. We'll also be following a couple of hashtags that relate to course topics, including an author of one of our books. But I'm using Twitter strictly as a tool for building personal learning networks and connecting with people and groups that I can't get into the classroom for face-to-face talks. I'll encourage students use it to continue class discussions once class is over. But I'm not sure that using it as the primary form of discussion in class is effective. There are just too many distractions (like the trending topics sidebar). Actually, the hype over the in-class backchannel has mostly been supplanted with a more sober approach, as I think many who have tried it have found that the cons outweigh the pros. (A major pro is that it allows the shyer students a forum.) But one of my goals is to teach students how to verbally communicate in groups, so I don't want to muddy that up with Twitter. If you're interested in Twitter in the classroom in action, there's a great video on YouTube about the Twitter experiment at UT Dallas."

There are PowerPoint templates to create and play your own version of Jeopardy. My *Business Law* class loves Jeopardy. I randomly divide them into teams of 3 or 4 people. Top two teams get bonus points on the next exam. I also include a "Grab Bag" category with miscellaneous questions about the college or about me. Another category I include is "Actual Test Questions." The students really perk up when they see that topic. It's not only fun and creative, but it's a great review.

A teacher said, "All of our classes at my university are offered online. One of the instructors of our PhD courses inaugurated a 'reflect and review' final post for each two-week module. These R&R posts have had the effect of a graduate seminar in that each student has the opportunity to review key ideas that struck him or her and to reflect on the applications of the ideas. The posts have helped us as instructors obtain a different perspective on what the students are really taking away from the course, not just what we read in their essays."

Media "Digital Participation"

Course-based Websites

Perhaps the easiest way to start incorporating the internet in your teaching is through a course-based website. These can range from the standard Blackboard, Canvas, or WebCT like options, to a webpage you create yourself, to a student-fueled site.

One forward-thinking teacher asked her current students to write down things they'd like to share with future students and then posted the responses on the class website, giving potential undergrads the student point of view. In a similar vein, another fan of the course website recommended you "write up how useful and important your course is, and how they'll use it in the future and post this information on your website. Remind them in class of this too."

Many teachers encourage utilization of the discussion functions provided by virtual learning environments (like Blackboard): "[I tell students:] Go to the library, find the physics section, find a book that is interesting to YOU, check the book out of the library. Post to WebCT's discussion forum your name and where you are from, the title and author of the book and why it interests you." What a great way to promote student interest in even the most challenging (or "boring" as the students may label it) subjects and then spread that interest around via online discussion.

Wikis and Blogs

Both teachers and students seem to enjoy the integration of wikis into a course. One student fondly recalled a course in which "a class wiki was set up where students earned points for posting relevant topical information," while an *Ethics* professor assigned a project to "create a wiki about a particular series that they'll decide on as a group in which they discuss the ethics of the series." Wikis allow the benefits of collaboration but from a distance and at the user's convenience. Students will feel more a part of the class and greatly appreciate the leeway.

I'll bet if you asked your class, "How many of you have a blog?" at least half the hands in the room would go up. Students may appear to not like writing, but what's more likely is they don't like the forced, formal writing structures courses tend to require. Blogging can be an excellent way to bridge the gap between required writing and engagement. This teacher has his students "respond to class content by researching and blogging on a mutual blog site" each week. Another teacher said students are required to "respond and comment on their classmates' observations (blogs). This adds to the classroom discussions as well as causes the students to have a common ground in cyberspace as well as a safe space to air their personal opinions without too much fear of argument at the onset."

Social Networking Sites Galore!
Your students are already familiar with Facebook and Twitter and use them on a regular basis, so why not parlay that familiarity into course engagement?

You can also create a course page in Facebook if you'd rather not force your students to exercise concision (those 140 Twitter characters can go by pretty quickly sometimes), and you'd like to take advantage of the vast number of options that site allows. Imagine assigning *English* students to play one of the site's word games and the highest score each week gets an extra quiz grade. A Facebook wall is also a great place to post reminders of upcoming due dates and maybe a Facebook Page only extra credit opportunity.

But maybe you're looking for a way to allow your students to contribute that doesn't require words? Start a class "bulletin" board on Pinterest. Not only can you pin anything you come across while browsing the web, but so can your students. Found a really great video that simplifies a rather complex *Physics* lesson? Pin it. Found an article that perfectly fits with what you and your economics class just discussed? Pin it. Encourage students to contribute quality pins by offering extra credit, or turn it into a competition: classmates can vote on the relevance of each other's pins, and the pins with the highest scores get prizes!

It's a YouTube World

No one site received more mention in my survey results than YouTube, so if you're not using it yet, you should be!

One digital enthusiast professed, "I am a huge fan of YouTube in the classroom—quick, easy resources to supplement my courses." A *History* teacher shared, "I have been adding YouTube clips to my online *American History* classes ever since I discovered that you can copy the 'Embed' HTML from any YouTube page, paste it into a Blackboard Announcement, click the HTML button below the announcement box, and voila!—you have the player embedded right in your Blackboard Announcements. It takes thirty seconds and is so cool. I spent a few hours tracking down short, silly history-related clips and setting up a whole semester's worth of 'YouTube Tuesdays.'" With literally billions of videos, there's no topic that isn't represented on YouTube, so there's no excuse for not adding a bit of visual magic to your course.

YouTube also works great for critiques and group activities. Create a course channel (set it to invite only), post videos of your students giving speeches and presentations, and have them critique each other. I had a colleague who divided her class into groups and assigned her students to create some sort of multimedia presentation (on any topic), which they would give to the class. One group decided to make a video presentation. They posted everything on YouTube so that each group member could have 24/7 access to the pieces of the presentation and the ability to make comments and suggestions. The student who was in charge of editing the final presentation then kept posting the video in its latest incarnation, making changes as different suggestions were approved by the group. The group never had to physically meet outside of class, but they seemed more involved and collaborative than those groups that did!

Don't forget that you can put yourself on YouTube too. I've seen *Math* teachers post videos of themselves tackling additional examples of the types of problems they taught their students in class and *Chemistry* teachers show off experiments at professional labs. I've yet to meet a teacher who complained about having too much time to cover all his lessons, and YouTube offers us all the opportunity of just a few more minutes to teach.

Other Internet Options
While YouTube and the social media sites are what all the buzz is about, they are FAR from the only useful online resources.

One particularly creative teacher uses a website to design crossword puzzles about course content: "I created crossword puzzles with terms from each chapter and used them as a little supplemental homework. Gives the students something different to look at and helps them become more confident with terms. Crossword Weaver is cheap shareware and allows you to put in terms and definitions to create a freeform puzzle."

Another teacher has students use a video creation website, complete with characters, called Xtranormal. Students "find a local problem, propose a solution for that, create an Xtranormal video explaining the problem and solution, and then write a justification essay arguing for the choices they made in the video." The tagline of Xtranormal is, "if you can type, you can make movies," so it's easy for students of all technological ability levels to use.

Sometimes you can even use sites to improve students' lifestyles. This student will never forget the far-reaching ramifications of one class: "For *Nutrition* we recorded everything we ate for three full days and entered the detailed information onto choosemyplate.com to be assessed and we got a very extensive feedback of our current nutrient intake. It made me alter my eating habits."

The Fiverr Challenge

There is a cool micro services website at www.fiverr.com. I came to class one day (*Social Media Marketing*) and said, "Today we're going to start with what I call 'The Fiverr Challege.' This site provides a variety of services for $5. You are allocated a budget of $50. In the next 30 minutes I want you to identify 10 "gigs" (as they are called) that can help you start a business." You can get simple logos, website templates, short video introductions, graphic art jobs, etc., all for $5. You'd be amazed at some of the interesting things you can get. I had a business department video introduction for a class produced (for just for $5). At the end of the allotted time I have students share with their neighbor the "deals" they found—all for fifty bucks!

Newsworthy (Old and New)

And of course the one thing the internet has in abundance is information—in every shape and form. This *Business* teacher tells his students to "keep checking cnn.com and similar news websites for something current, and discuss the business ramifications. They need not be specifically 'business' issues. For example, a hurricane is heading for the mainland; what's going to happen in the marketplace?" He goes on to suggest, "You could begin each class with such a discussion. You could have the students identify topics for discussion—everyone bring in a 'hot' news story of the day." But, as this *History* teacher demonstrates, news sites aren't the only place to get information: "For *American History* there are so many

Media "Digital Participation"

great things online—podcasts such as TalkingHistory.org, interviews with authors, videos of history presentations at WGBH in Boston and other places like the Library of Congress, historic films at Archive.org and Google Video, history-themed cartoons and commercials at YouTube, and tons of primary sources, from the History Matters site to Google Book Search. Every week and in all my classes I use Internet resources."

The results of media-themed projects are almost universally positive, and here are just a few more results that confirm exactly that:

"I was a teaching assistant leading a *Communications 101* discussion group. At the end of the quarter, I asked students to bring in media or communications that they had made. The stuff people brought in moved the group so much and it became very emotional. One girl brought in a video she made to raise money for AIDS; another male student brought in a song he produced. It was awesome to see how much passion and energy they put into these creative outputs."

"We had to make a commercial for our research project and I did a commercial about the Jersey Shore!"

"I teach *Social Media and Cloud Computing* at a large community and technical college in Cincinnati. One of the 'capstone' projects is the development and publishing of an infographic that is a working résumé for the student. We went to a few websites and looked these up, then students were asked to create one. I then found an HR professional to 'rate' these, and students received grades accordingly. Fun and informative!"

While I've enjoyed sharing the best "Digital Participation" responses from my research, I want to make sure you leave this chapter asking yourself one very important question—what are the possibilities? These ideas are far from all there are, and you are limited only by your own drive and imagination. Why not take a minute right now and Google one of your course topics? You could spend days, weeks, or even months sifting through all the engaging internet options, and that's only one type of media! For every medium or type of technology, ask yourself, "How can I use this?" We tell students to never stop asking questions, so we need to take our own advice! Only by continuing to ask questions can we continue to discover answers. I've given you a few answers to the "What are the possibilities?" question, but the rest are up to you!

Twitter Summary:

Discover and embrace technological advances and resources to support, compliment and accelerate student engagement and learning.

Chapter 7

Beginning and Ending With a Bang

A significant number of respondents mentioned activities or principles that related directly to either the first or last day of class, so I decided to dedicate a chapter specifically to the two (arguably) most important days of the semester. What kind of Welcome Wagon have you got planned for the first day of class? Are you willing to shelve some of what you normally do? What can you do to win the enthusiastic participation of your students?

Art of the Start

One teacher imparted, "Students make up their minds about a teacher and class in the first THIRTY SECONDS or less of the first class," so make the most of it! Address Whatever Your Name Is early and often. Don't let the masters of avoidance look the other way.

The sweetest word a person ever hears is the sound of their name. I know you've got a lot of names to learn, but it'll definitely be worth the investment. Many of you can download a photo class roll. I'll surprise many of my students and call them by name on the first day of class. It takes a little time and effort. Another thing I've done on day one to get them up and moving is ask them to write their name, hometown and a hobby of theirs on the board. I have 3 walls that have whiteboard and many multi-colored markers placed around the room so there isn't much congestion at the board. There is something about seeing your own name on the board.

I know some teachers who will simply hand out a syllabus and say "get the book and be prepared for next time." Other teachers dive right in to delivering content (starting the "informational deluge" right out of the gate). Both of these options (and many more) represent a major lost opportunity.

> **Syllabus Tip**
> Put "student hours" on your syllabus (and then your door) instead of "office hours." You'll come across as more inviting and welcoming of student visitors. Who knows, maybe they'll stop by just to chitchat!

The ideal first hour, according to my research, will be unusual, include some "getting acquainted" elements (you'll see how these can be 'relevant' getting-acquainted ideas), give an overview of your plan for the course and its real-world relevancy, AND end just a little early (big surprise there).

But first, let's take a look at something you can do before class even *starts* that first day (and every day for that matter).

The Value of Chitchat

I want to address one teacher's response because it really resonated with me—and contained a conclusion it took

Beginning and Ending With a Bang

me a number of years to realize on my own! (Oh, how I wish I had completed this survey earlier in my career.) This teacher heartily recommended getting to class five to ten minutes early to engage in chitchat with students; simple right? And this teacher also provided a wonderful list of the benefits he experienced from doing just that:

- I had an easier time remembering more about students and their work.
- After a week or so the students relaxed; they talked more openly to me before, during, and after class. My own presentations to the class and discussions became more relaxed as well.
- More students arrived on time. (I suspect because they began to feel I was starting "right on" the posted start time.)
- More students showed up during my office hours.
- Students seemed to interact more with one another.
- Overall attendance and participation went up.
- The results were close to the same in three different classes.

I can tell you from personal experience that this teacher's recommendation is right on, so why not start utilizing the power of chitchat right from the beginning? Plus, students generally won't be expecting such informal friendliness the first day (teachers are usually too busy trying to appear no nonsense and tough, so that students won't try to take advantage of our true, easy-going natures from the get-go); points for hitting the "unusual" target before class even begins!

Quick Student Engagement Ideas for Busy Teachers

Unexpected Solutions

Other unusual first options could include taking a field trip, the do-it-yourself syllabus, or showing students "the wrong way."

Just like Monty Python's Spanish Inquisition, no one expects a field trip on the first day! You don't have to go far either. If the weather allows, walk your class to a nice outdoor spot for the getting acquainted activity. If several of your assignments will send them to the campus library, why not remind them of where it is during the last five to ten minutes of class? If you'd prefer to make it a challenge, you could always enlist the help of the friendly library staff and tell your students their first day's homework is in the library, so go find it! If you do go the field trip route, try to wait at least ten minutes into class to depart, and don't forget to leave a note for any latecomers!

I'd never heard about a DIY syllabus until a student respondent told about his experience: The teacher walked into the first day of class and handed out a "syllabus" that included the usual header information, a list of books, and two blank pages. "What the heck?" the students asked. The teacher told the students he was tired of doing all the work around here; "You guys need to design the class." He continued on, "We need forty pages of writing, a way of making sure you are actually doing all the reading, and a combination of discussions, student presentations, film, field trips, and guest lecturers. Oh, and we need a grading scheme—what percentage of your grade goes where. Now if you'll excuse me I haven't had

Beginning and Ending With a Bang

my coffee—I'll be back in twenty minutes or so. Get to work!"

As you may have guessed, the students hadn't quite achieved perfection by the time the teacher returned. They did, however, have enough material to create (with a little professorial assistance) a perfectly workable syllabus for the course—a course they now felt belonged to them.

I've successfully used this several times. The key takeaway is that students feel ownership and buy-in. Any time students can be involved in the direction of their education learning is magnified.

How about taking everything you intend to teach your students and doing it the wrong way? "One . . . activity I have used is . . . giving an oral presentation in which I do everything wrong: I dress inappropriately, I chew gum and blow bubbles, I am disorganized, I don't make eye contact, my PowerPoint slides are hideous, I pace, I use nervous mannerisms, I talk too long, I mumble, etc., etc." Students are then asked to point out what the teacher did wrong. It's not only a fun and entertaining activity, but it also allows the teacher to gauge the overall level of class knowledge.

And if you'd like to take this activity to a higher level, do the same thing on the *last* day of class. Allowing students to point out all the "wrong" elements *then* will give them a chance to show off and take pride in all they've learned. Compare how many "wrong" things they pointed out the first day with the last day; students love self-evident representations of their own progress and achievements. (Just make sure you don't tell them all the "this was wrong" answers on the first day if you're planning to use the "bookends" version of this activity—that's what the rest of the semester is for!)

Let's Get Acquainted

Now that you have, hopefully, surprised your students into attention, it's time for everyone to become acquainted—and that includes YOU. Too often I see teachers having their students play "getting to know you games," but not engaging in them themselves. Another missed opportunity!

Acquaintance-making activities don't have to be complex. One teacher suggested that any activity in which "each person participates and shares something significant about the class topic in that person's own personal life" will work. Of course if a student is having a little trouble figuring out how the course material will apply to his or her life (or "all the good answers have been taken"), feel free to step in and Socratic method a response from him or her. And when it's your turn, this teacher has some good advice for you: "Nothing establishes your credentials as one human among others better than an anecdote that is funny at your own expense."

I really enjoyed one crafty teacher's idea to have students "design a motivational poster on the first day of class in groups in order to get to know other people fast." If you want to take the assignment a step further, offer them the option to make a "demotivational" poster (and show them a few of the humorous examples on the internet.) It would be interesting to see which groups decided to be inspirational and which ones decided to be funny—though I have no doubt you'd eventually end up with a group that managed both!

The Big Picture

Another great first day/week activity I call the *Big Picture*. This is how it works. I place large, poster-sized sheets of paper (with sticky) scattered around the room. I have students draw a line across their sheet of paper (about half way down). On the top half of the sheet I want you to draw (I tell them) who you are, but you can't use any words or numbers—just pictures.

They draw pictures that attempt to represent elements of their life. After several minutes I ask them to now draw on the bottom half of their sheet things that represent where they are going in life. Once this is complete I have students begin to pair up and explain their *Big Picture*. I have them trade partners several times to share pictures. This is a great kick-off activity that facilitates the free-flow of information as we begin course content.

And if you're even the slightest bit reluctant to include an acquaintance-building activity into your first day schedule, keep this student's confession in mind: "Even though I hate them at first, I really do enjoy being forced at the first class period of a semester to get to know those around me."

Traffic Jam is a great activity that teaches teamwork, communication, leadership, problem solving and a fun way to get acquainted. It is a little complicated to explain, but if you Google "traffic jam experiential exercise" or "traffic jam team building game" you will find the instructions as well as the solution. It basically involves teams of 6 or 8 standing on either paper plates or sheets of paper attempting to flip half the team with the other half of the team with only 2 valid forward moves. You may have to give a couple of the first steps of the solution if teams start to get too frustrated.

54

This may be a little difficult to understand, but it's worth the mental sweat. I call it *Numbers*. There is a sheet with 54 numbers on it in different fonts, sizes and locations. You can either pass out a paper sheet or show this on your overhead screen. If you pass the paper out physically instruct students to place the sheet face down and not look at the printed side. Their instructions are to find as many numbers as possible (in ascending order) in one minute. I instruct students to look for the first number, point at it and say out loud "one." Then, look for, point at and say out loud "two," etc. Continue through number 54. If you get to number 54 in 60 seconds (which you won't I tell them) then start back over with number one. "Are my instructions clear?" I ask them.

Now, here is the important part. I assign two or three people to turn their chairs around facing the back wall and sit this first round out. Then, as I start the rest of the class with "go" I quietly make my way to the back of the room and give those sitting out the "pattern." Here is the pattern. If you picture your paper in nine quadrants (three across and three down) that is the pattern. In the top-left quadrant you'll find number one. In the top-middle quadrant you'll find number two. In the top-right quadrant you'll find number three. In the middle-left quadrant you'll find number four, etc. After you find number nine in the bottom-right quadrant you'll return to the top-left quadrant to find what number? Number 10.

So, after the first round (be sure to watch your clock to say "stop" after 60 seconds) I ask how it went and what can you do to increase your speed. I call on several people (my test group) and ask them to share with the class their score. I say if this exercise represents productivity, what can we do to be more productive? Ok, let's try it again and see if you can improve your score.

At the end of this round I call on my test group again and they usually realize some meager gains. Then I ask my two people who sat out the first round. They usually get in the upper 40's if not all the way to 54 in 60 seconds. The rest of the class perks up and looks a little surprised and doubtful that the scores were accurate. How can that be I ask the class?

Then I ask one of the people that knew the pattern to tell the rest of the class how they can be "exceptional" too. The class is excited with the new-found pattern and we do one final round. Many are proud to report they got all the way to number 54 and, in some cases, continue even higher.

I conclude with a discussion of the power of information; how a little information can be extremely powerful and in this case, much more productive. It's a very effective and engaging exercise.

Quick Student Engagement Ideas for Busy Teachers

Bring On the Overview

The days when giving out the syllabus was "all the overview a student needs" are gone (if they ever really existed). Students need—and deserve—a more thorough explanation of the course and, as one teacher put it, "Professors must 'sell' why their class is important."

A student suggested we ask our classes the following first day questions: "1) What do you hope to learn from this class? 2) What is an experience related to this class from your own history? 3) Give an example from a book, movie, or television show that is related to this class and why you make that connection. 4) If you had the opportunity to spend the day with a professional who is knowledgeable in this area, what kind of professional would you choose and why?" Not only does this course of questioning allow teachers to get a better idea of students' pre-conceived notions of the class, but it also gets students thinking in depth about the course from the beginning.

One professor states that in addition to a list of questions similar to the above, "I have also started asking them 'What can you do to succeed in the course?' and 'What can I do to help you succeed in the course?' This makes them think at least a little about the fact that their success will in large part depend on what they do. It also can bring up a few suggestions that I may incorporate in class when they are reasonable."

Share Early

Another teacher has students "tell one thing they are excited about, then in another round one thing they are

Beginning and Ending With a Bang

nervous about concerning the course." He says he starts it off until people get warmed up, saying something like, "I'm excited to share some new ideas from this *Social Media* class that can help you find a job. Now, I'm a little nervous about learning the forty names of my students in this class." He also allows follow-up comments or questions after each student shares his or her excitement and concern, and addresses many things himself. This allows for calming fears, correcting misconceptions, and really telling students what they actually WANT to know.

When offering an overview of the future of your course, one of the most useful things you can do is establish what students can do to contribute to a good discussion in your class. This teacher suggests you "tell them that while it's your job to manage discussions, it's their job to contribute productively. Take a couple of minutes to brainstorm what makes a discussion engaging, useful, and productive. Then pick the top three or so characteristics of productive contributions. Have the students write down those discussion guidelines and keep them in mind when they make comments in class." A different option could be to "discuss successful and not-so-successful classes that they have had in the past, and to speculate and make conclusions."

Not only are you showing you care about what your students consider successful and unsuccessful teaching methods, you can also discover some pretty good ideas!

Let's review that formula for a successful and engaging first day one more time: Start off with a bang (first 30 seconds), get acquainted (yet make it relate to the course content), express feelings about the content (from both sides), and end early (but not too early). Piece of cake now, right?

Killer Conclusions

Let's assume you followed the above recipe for a superb first day; a semester (and an untold amount of grading) later you're faced with the equally significant final day. Will you march them majestically out the front door pondering some of life's deepest secrets or will you quietly slip out the backdoor before they even know you're gone?

Okaay, so you may not be able to go the "life's deepest secrets" route, but you can leave a lasting impression that will help to cement all they learned in your class. And isn't that really our final goal? Not just that they learn, but that they *retain* what they learn. We want life-long students of learning.

Letter to Future Students (by students)
One of the best ways to have students acknowledge what they've learned and how hard they've worked is to have them create a message to share with future students, like this teacher: "On the last day of class I have students write a letter to future students in the class telling them what to expect. How should they study? What challenges will they face in studying? Which concepts and units are the most exciting, etc.?"

Another teacher who used a similar activity shared, "It was really heartwarming to see them come up with things like, 'Have faith in yourself. You can do this.' or

'This class is hard but totally worth it!' or 'This class will really help you be open-minded—be ready to learn a lot!'

It is a good way to synthesize the things they'd learned in the class and it gave the students a chance to reflect on how far they'd come, and how much more confident they were. Then it is a great preview of things to come to hand out to your new class."

I used this last semester and it was a very powerful reflective exercise. I then passed those letters on to my new semester students. If things have gone amazingly well in your class that semester then your students become your fans and write to their peers about the fun and exciting things they have to look forward to. These mini-testimonials were equally powerful bookends of my classes.

Why didn't we get one?

Yesterday I myself handed out lined paper and asked my *Business Law* class to draft a letter to next semester's students. One student spoke up and asked, "Why didn't we get a letter?" I replied, "Because I just thought of it this semester." Coming across the suggestion in my research did indeed make me think of it! To sooth any hurt feelings, I continued, "But don't worry, those of you who fail and have to retake my class will absolutely get a letter next semester!" The class laughs hard.

Toys, Games and Food (again)

Here is an interactive idea to culminate the end of a class, "As a final in a *Career* class, we played 'Charades,' acting out different vocations, majors, occupations, careers. Once the 'job' was guessed, details about the career were discussed: Salary, education, prognosis for the future, etc." It may seem a little elementary at first, but it sounds fun and purposeful.

Service Learning symbolism
If you'd like to go the more creative route, you could follow this teacher's lead: "At the final class in a *Service Learning* course, I had students use Play-Doh to construct something that captured symbolically what they had gained from their service learning projects." This also allows students to create something very personal as they won't have to make sure what they sculpt is something a future student can understand. It also makes for a nice keepsake to help them remember the course. (Or a little jar of Play-Doh to remember the course for those students who can't bear to let it dry out.)

Wine and Cheese Poster Session
You may remember the power of food from the materials chapter, well it's just as (if not more) powerful that last day of class! For an age-appropriate class, you could always try this teacher's idea: "In my *Research* course, we are having a wine-and-cheese poster session. . . . They've worked hard this semester on their projects and we spent the last week constructing posters, so this poster session is really just a chance to show off what they've learned and socialize a bit. I'm looking forward to it—probably as much as or more than they are!"

Potluck
You could always try for a state-food and game themed meeting like this *English* teacher: "Every semester we

Beginning and Ending With a Bang

have a Spud Party; here in Idaho, spuds (or potatoes) are essential to the economy. The students bring the toppings and I bake the spuds. We sit in a circle and play The Adverb game (acting out adverbs without speaking), and the definition game (Call My Bluff)."

Possibly the most popular food-themed final class, however, is the potluck: "In my *Latin American History* courses we have a Latin-themed potluck on the last day. I link some relevant recipe websites and allow those who just can't cook to bring something from a local bodega. It is always a huge hit!"

Another teacher candidly shares, "I usually hold a potluck. Students love that, and I get a great turnout. We review and eat and laugh and it's really a good time. It also encourages students to come to the review. After each one, I swear I'll never do it again, but I find it quite beneficial for everyone." Join the party!

Whatever memorable and innovative activity you decide on, make your last class day an engaging celebration of the days that came before it!

Capitalize on the greatest two days of the semester for a tremendous start and conclusion of your class!

A happy ending—or just the beginning?

Twitter Summary:

Strategically prepare for and capitalize on the two most valuable days of the semester. Ignite a learning tone for the semester and beyond.

Chapter 8

In Conclusion

I truly hope I've shown you how to become a better teacher—not just through collected suggestions and examples, but through my encouraging you to make much in this book your own. The Enterprising Engagement Model is just that—a model. It's not a dictate, a decree, or even a list of instructions; it's a framework and a set of moldable ideas just waiting for you to get your mental hands on—something to be mixed with your own thoughts, ideas, and experiences and turned into educational magic.

Alvin Toffler said, "The illiterate of the 21st century will not be those who cannot read or write, but those who cannot learn, unlearn, and relearn." I know we can learn. The question is, can we teachers "unlearn and relearn?" Much of what we have learned about teaching isn't working—it isn't encouraging engagement or producing students who actually retain what they learn in our classes. To continue on in our current manner, using the same old methods, will make us "illiterate" indeed. There is, however, a cost of "good teaching." We must be willing to devote time and effort to creating and carrying out the activities and exercises that will take our teaching to a higher level—that will help us to offer a genuinely *higher* education.

Quick Student Engagement Ideas for Busy Teachers

But don't think that you have to begin your quest for effective engagement with some grand gesture or complete pedagogical upheaval. All you need to do is something, *anything*. Start small and begin practicing. I've given you hundreds of ideas you can use as jumping off points. You don't have to immediately begin pumping out innovative genius, but that should be your end goal (well, not necessarily the genius part, but definitely the innovative part). The harder you try, the more you practice, and the more you experience, the more you will be able to develop further insight on innovative and engaging classroom (and beyond) activities. Part of being a great teacher is recognizing that just like your students, **you** always have something to learn. Then, action follows thought.

A question everyone should ask himself, no matter his profession, is "what can I do to get better?" Never stop asking yourself, "What are the possibilities in and beyond my classroom?" Only when we stop asking questions do we stop learning, and as teachers we cannot afford to *ever* stop learning—especially about teaching. The second you think you've finally got this teaching thing down perfect is the second you sink into stagnation, and the second innovation begins to die. Then it's only a hop, skip, and a jump to reverting back to the good old reliable deluge of lecture.

> The class is quiet—a little distant at first. I have to do some heavy lifting to bring them back. A few now speak up. Others begin to *get it* and jump into the verbal blitz. It gets better. Everybody now seems to be on board. I'm riding high as the class

In Conclusion

draws to a close. It took some work, but it was worth it. Things finally clicked. My students *got it*. The delivery vehicle I chose helped me connect. My students seemed to be screaming, "Give me more! Bring it on!" I feel like a real teacher. I find great purpose in my classroom. I love being a teacher!

How do we make this happen in our classrooms? Perhaps we schedule a faculty retreat to brainstorm and share best practices. Innovation and engaged teaching should always be on our agendas (every agenda). Perhaps you can gather your colleagues for a book discussion and ask them to bring one example of something they've done differently as a result of reading this book. The material in this book aligns well with your institutional mission and goals.

As I stated earlier, I am not a poor teacher; I am a rich teacher—we all are. We have the greatest job in the world—a job that offers us the opportunity to inspire, shape, and influence lives. And we need to ensure we are doing that job as well as we possibly can with as much passion as we can offer.

True story (last one). On a recent trip with my family we ventured down a familiar road that led us to a destination we've visited many times before. This place is off the beaten path a little, so there are several ways to get there, but we opted for our normal route—seeing the same old street signs, passing the same old scenery, and following the same old pattern.

Quick Student Engagement Ideas for Busy Teachers

I had heard about a "short-cut," a right-hand turn that might get us to our destination quicker. Many times as I passed that right turn I would briefly think about giving it a try, but would then decide, "Not today." (Not today; how often do we say that?)

On an even more recent trip to that same destination, I finally committed to taking that short-cut and seeing where it would take us; "not today" became, "yes, TODAY." I bravely broke my routine and chose to travel a new path—a path I hadn't taken before. Yes, it took a little courage. I finally turned right, and I was pleasantly surprised. The road was smoother than I thought, and the scenery was even better. My new-found path took me to places along the way that I had never been to before, and I still saved time, arriving at my destination quicker than ever before.

I hope you'll consider a new path. Give it a try.

I know as busy teachers your time is valuable and limited, so I hope you'll use the research I've done as a short-cut to new ideas—new ideas that can take you to exciting new places of learning while still reaching the end goals of engagement and retention.

It's time to make that "right" turn and discover your own new path—the first of many. Best of luck to you great teachers of the world!

Appendix: Cheat Sheet (summary list)

Put an "**X**" in the box of ideas you'd definitely like to do (or do more of) in your classes. Put a forward slash "/" (half an "X") in the box if the idea might be a possibility (something you'd like to consider). Later if it is something you want to add, you can complete the "X" by putting a backward slash "\".

MOVEMENT *"Less Seat Time"*

__ **MOTION CREATES EMOTION** (pair share, small groups, jigsaw learning method, carousel learning method, etc.) page 38

__ **SPEED LEARNING** (like speed dating, what did you grasp from the reading) page 39

__ **JIGSAW LEARNING STATIONS** (the jigsaw learning method or how to create subject matter experts) page 38

__ **COMMUNITY EVENT** (attend a community event you wouldn't normally attend—write before and after the event) page 52

__ **UNCONVENTIONAL QUIZZES** (Walmart quiz: find the answers at the store) page 49

Quick Student Engagement Ideas for Busy Teachers

- __ **WALK THE ROOM** (motion creates emotion) page 33
- __ **TURN CHAIRS INWARD** (creating a horseshoe setting if possible, students see more student faces) page 27
- __ **LOCAL CEMETERY** (visit and then write about the family, community) page 47
- __ **MEANINGFUL MOVEMENT** (accounting balance sheet, business law process) page 43
- __ **WHITEBOARDS ON ALL FOUR CLASSROOM WALLS** (for more student involvement and expression) page 37
- __ **SCAVENGER HUNT** (library or campus) page 48
- __ **EDUCATIONAL GRAFFITI WALL** (highlight educational concepts in a casual yet visible manner, whiteboards, poster boards) page 41
- __ **WHERE DO YOU STAND?** (vote with your feet, controversial statements on either side of the room, explore the issues by taking sides literally) page 36
- __ **FACULTY RETREAT** (share your own "best practices") page 135
- __ **DIVIDE AND CONQUER** (to divide class into discussion groups: hand clasp, odd/even birthdays, age, height, last time you went to the movies, etc.) page 38
- __ **THE AMERICAN DREAM** (don't just talk business—start one!) page 51
- __ **COMMUNITY MARKETING HELP** (helping local business) page 53
- __ **TAKE ME HOME** (students to teacher's home) page 56
- __ **THE GREAT OUTDOORS** (rope course, yurts, cross country skiing, reading and rappelling) page 48

Cheat Sheet

- **GUERILLA THEATER** (costume design, community plays and on campus) page 54
- **HIDDEN OBJECTS** (positive/negative feedback) page 44
- **COMMUNITY BUDGET CHALLENGE** (real-world financial challenge and contribution) page 52
- **ENTREPRENEUR CHALLENGE** (for a good cause) page 55
- **CAROUSEL LEARNING METHOD** (movement method with learning stations) page 39
- **GENDER BIAS** (exploring gender learning and expression differences) page 43
- **SHAPING OR MOLDING** (instrumental positive and negative cues) page 44
- **ENGINEERING OUTREACH PROJECT** (teaching science or engineering at the local school) page 53
- **FROM THE CHEAP SEATS** (surprise your students by sitting and speaking on their level) page 34
- **EQUINE-FACILITATED LEARNING** (horses, barns and education) page 48
- **TALKING TO ONE** (when you talk to one you talk to all) page 34
- **YOU BE THE JURY** (you may never be an attorney, but critical thinker yes) page 41
- **I DON'T THINK SO** (the stimulating effect of debates) page 41
- **DONDE ESTA MI ZAPATO** (a Spanish lesson on possession) page 45
- **WHEELCHAIR MOVEMENT** (practice moving patient to dental chair) page 45

Quick Student Engagement Ideas for Busy Teachers

- __ **STEP OUTSIDE FOR A MOMENT** (read account of Mt. Everest ascent) page 46
- __ **FANTASTIC FIELD DAY** (physical education event involving the local school) page 56
- __ **NO YELLOW BUS FIELD TRIP** (a visit to the Human Resource office) page 46
- __ **FOOTBALL DECIBELS** (noise measurements at BYU football game) page 50
- __ **DIRTY WORLD** (bacteria and cotton swabs) page 51
- __ **ANGEL INVESTORS** (best voted plan gets funded) page 51
- __ **MORE FIELD TRIPS** (Business, communication, leadership) page 48
- __ **SERVICE LEARNING** (a life lesson learned while giving back) page 54
- __ **PUZZLE PIECES** (puzzle piece terms and answers—students with terms try to find right students with definition on their puzzle pieces) page 37
- __ **EDUCATIONAL CRUISE** (business division-learning on the open seas) page 59
- __ **ELEVATOR PITCH** (a short, concise summary of key points of a particular topic in a competitive fashion) page 36
- __ **BUSINESS SCAVENGER HUNT** (send them downtown for the answers) page 49
- __ **THE CULTURE OF** (learned culture of the teacher) page 58
- __ **COMMUNITY PLAY** (costume design) page 53
- __ **HUMAN ARCH** (Romanesque and Gothic arches) page 43

Cheat Sheet

- **QUIZ, QUIZ, TRADE** (trading index card quiz questions) page 42
- **CLASSMATE INTERVIEWS** (each person interprets history a little differently) page 42
- **MBA IN THE WOODS** (basic communication and team building) page 48
- **SPEEDY SME'S** (Subject Matter Experts: sharing the collective knowledge and demonstrate the value of learner participation, share information quickly on a variety of topics) page 38
- **THE JOB YOU LOVE** (or hate, a reflective assessment exploring the reasons why) page 40
- **VOTE WITH YOUR FEET** (physically show me how you feel by where you stand) page 35

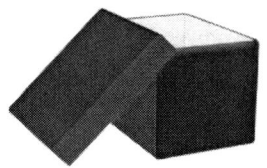

MATERIAL *"Show-'N'-Tell"*

- **IN THE NEWS** (article analysis, read and discuss current affairs and keep abreast of developments that impact the industry, students write reflection papers about the article) page 71

Quick Student Engagement Ideas for Busy Teachers

- __ **TINKER TOYS** (build something then write instruction manual on how to build it) page 62
- __ **DEAD OR ALIVE** (biology teacher brings random things to quiz students if it's dead or alive) page 69
- __ **STAR POWER** (non-computer based simulation of an organization where leaders are given power to change the rules) page 63
- __ **YO-YO VISUALS** (the power and recall of visual teaching devices) page 64
- __ **PAPER BALL FIGHT** (write misperceptions, stereotypes, or fallacies of your topic, then paper ball fight, then "throw away" the bad information) page 71
- __ **INDEX CARDS** (the good—something learned today, the bad–didn't quite understand, also "yes" and "no" cards for more participation) page 72
- __ **DOUGHNUT AUCTION** (economics auction to illustrate supply and demand) page 67
- __ **HARD CANDY** (a teacher gives out Smarties and Nerds, or how about Dum Dums and Airheads?) page 68
- __ **POTLUCK REVIEW** (feed the body and the mind) page 66
- __ **LEARNING CONNECTIONS** (build upon your classmate's contribution) page 74
- __ **WHAT'S IN YOUR WALLET** (staged introduction for observation and inference writing assignment) page 66
- __ **JUST BALLS** (conjugate verbs and x-axis illustration) page 62
- __ **POSITION PAPERS** (a written personal opinion on relevant topic) page 71

Cheat Sheet

- **BUILD A TOWER** (many learning outcomes with a simple marshmallow and toothpick assignment) page 68
- **PANCAKES** (chemistry illustration for students) page 66
- **M&M'S** (chi-square and distribution exercises based on colored candies) page 67
- **TERMITES** (termites and ink analysis) page 70
- **HYDROGEN-PROPELLED ROCKETS** (you'll be the most popular teacher on campus) page 69
- **DRESS UP** (hippies, mad scientist and the integral man) page 65
- **HOME-BAKED GOODS** (intentional assignment both good and good for you) page 67
- **CHEMICAL REACTIONS** (shake well then back up) page 68
- **PACKAGING** (consumer goods analysis) page 74
- **TREAT SIGN-UP** (voluntary assignment especially for the early morning class) page 67
- **EVOLUTIONAL TREE** (build one with a variety of toys) page 62
- **THE GAME OF LIFE** (the real game of life) page 63
- **YOU'VE RUINED MY WEEKEND** (how hard is your class) page 72
- **WHO WANTS TO BE A...?** (game show quiz or exam review) page 63

MINDFULNESS *"Flex Your Mind Muscle"*

- __ **1-MINUTE PAPER** (A small investment of time can yield contemplative thought and reflection: what did you learn today? About 5-10 minutes before class ends. Reduce, review, recite, recall) page 84
- __ **FABULOUS FINAL FIVE MINUTES** (of every class period, structured conclusions for greater impact) page 99
- __ **GOOGLE 20% Rule** (allow students to choose where they will spend 20% of their learning time and what they will work on, and where 20% of their grade will come from) page 26
- __ **TOP 10 LIST** (a fun and contemporary way to create a review list or key learning points in a creative way) page 85
- __ **RESPONSE PAPER** (what did you learn either from article or text? 1 paragraph "play by play" and 1 paragraph "color") page 83
- __ **FREE WRITE** (students free-write for 5 minutes about a topic, paper is passed to next student who continues to write on the new topic) page 83
- __ **SIX-WORD STORY** (six-word stories, value statements, or review statements) page 100

Cheat Sheet

- **THE DEBRIEF** (the most important thing after a learning activity is to discuss what just happened and what is the application) page 28
- **PUBLIC SERVICE AD CAMPAIGN** (develop a public service ad campaign to help promote a cause or reading before class) page 100
- **STORYLINE** (UPS-the power of stories) page 98
- **TELL ME A STORY** (don't be afraid to let your personal side show for greater impact and connection) page 98
- **DEFINING A GREAT CUSTOMER EXPERIENCE** (What does it LOOK, FEEL, SOUND like? Create a list of tangible, observable components of a great customer service experience) page 85
- **YOU CAN NEGOTIATE ANYTHING** (the intense and very competitive nature of negotiation is explored through real-world classroom stakes) page 97
- **LET IT STORM** (the amazing power of brainstorming—Orville Redenbacher) page 97
- **WE ALL ARE DIFFERENT** (explore differences and similarities through words…new insights and connections) page 90
- **THE BEST COLOR EYES** (discrimination and perspective, green eyes can leave early) page 90
- **THE REAL WORLD** (UPS, Smith Corona, Netflix, Ebay: from casual observation to case studies) page 98
- **WHAT HAVE WE LEARNED TODAY?** (summarize, reduce, package) page 78
- **10 MINUTES LEFT…** (you may leave after 3 questions from the audience) page 79

Quick Student Engagement Ideas for Busy Teachers

- **CONTROVERSIAL ISSUES** (abolish sales tax and replace by what?) page 88
- **OWNERSHIP** (what do you want to do today?) page 85
- **STUDENT-WRITTEN QUIZZES AND EXAMS** (let them do the work and remember more) page 86
- **QUIZ EXCHANGE** (small student groups write quiz then exchange) page 87
- **GET IT IN WRITING** (rather than talk about it, write about what you learned) page 81
- **RESPONSE PAPER** (write a paper in response to a controversial issue the class is dealing with) page 88
- **PEER PAPER** (honest student peer feedback on classmates, possible Johari Window application) page 95
- **HEALTH ASSESSMENT** (beneficial health review) page 93
- **POSITION PAPER** (written position paper on assigned reading) page 80
- **HOW MUCH MONEY WOULD IT TAKE?** (an ethical test assessing and examining your "purchasing power") page 94
- **FUNNY PAPERS** (a serious analysis) page 96
- **MASS OF THE SUN** (is there really enough information to compute this?) page 97
- **FAMILY BUDGET** (small groups given different dollar amounts to formulate different budgets) page 89
- **DIFFICULT PERSON** (how to deal with) page 92
- **HOLOCAUST LETTER** (read without introduction for students to guess the unexpected scenario) page 91
- **THE THEORY OF A FIRM** (what is the product and who is the customer?) page 91

Cheat Sheet

- **THE RULES OF LAW** (assigned authority determines rules of class conduct) page 92
- **WRITER, READER, DOER** (teams of three with different assigned limitations) page 80
- **ONE WORD AT A TIME** (a team of two communicates alternating a word at a time) page 101
- **SHADOWED** (students assigned to observe classmate for writing assignment) page 80
- **THE POWER OF QUESTIONS** (greater learning by asking the right questions) page 78
- **FISH BOWL TRIVIA** (students turn in 3X5 cards with question on one side and answer on the other, then compete as teams and the work has been done for you) page 86
- **ON TRIAL** (put a character from a novel on trial) page 88
- **RESPONSE TO RESPONSE** (student peer responses and feedback) page 96
- **GROUP SUMMARIES** (a different kind of review) page 82
- **5 MINUTE WRITING** (response to question at beginning of class) pager 82
- **REGULATORY TESTIMONY** (create your own trial) page 89
- **WHAT DO YOU THINK?** (the four most important words you'll ever say) page 77
- **PERFECT INTEGRITY** (for three days, then what you learned) page 93
- **SELF-IMPROVEMENT** (an outside book for personal development) page 94
- **BOOK PILE** (pick your reading from the pile) page 95

Quick Student Engagement Ideas for Busy Teachers

- __ **HOW TO GET STUDENTS TO READ THEIR BOOK** (finally the answer) page 9
- __ **PERIODIC PAUSES** (if you do happen to lecture) page 13
- __ **PATTERN INTERRUPT** (interval change to maintain interest) page 20

MEDIA *"Digital Participation"*

- __ **LIGHTS, CAMERA, ACTION** (the YouTube phenomenon: the power of short video) page 111
- __ **JEOPARDY** (increase learner engagement through the use of learning games and simulations) page 108
- __ **BLOG** (assign to blog on a mutual website) page 110
- __ **PODCAST** (assign industry podcasts) page 104
- __ **TWITTER** (Twitter participation, with Twitter there are no "back rows") page 107
- __ **CROSSWORD PUZZLE** (websites to create your own crossword puzzles for your discipline) page 113
- __ **GOOGLE DOCS** (create, share, collaborate on-line) page 104

Cheat Sheet

- **XTRANORMAL** ("if you can type you can make a movie") page 113
- **HOW HAS TECHNOLOGY CHANGED YOUR LIFE?** (a reflective assignment and prediction of future possibilities) page 103
- **VIDEO EMBEDS IN BLACKBOARD** (an easy way to incorporate web videos into your learning system) page 111
- **ALTERED EATING HABITS** (analysis website changes eating patterns) page 113
- **CELL PHONE APP** (application that selects random student names to call on) page 106
- **CELL PHONE POLLING** (in class polling options with cell phones and websites) page 106
- **BUSINESS NEWS WEBSITES** (numerous discipline-specific websites for relevant content) page 114
- **CREATE A CLASS WIKI** (an interesting class technology resource project) page 109
- **MEDIA PROJECT** (final meaningful mixed media project) page 115
- **INFOGRAPHIC** (students prepare an infographic) page 115
- **THERE'S AN APP FOR THAT** (look on-line for scores of educational apps) page 106
- **SKIM THE READING, POST QUESTION TO BLACKBOARD** (student questions are posted to blackboard for discussion) page 109
- **TEXT ME** (about class) page 106
- **EVEN PINTEREST** (pin me learning) page 111
- **THE FIVERR CHALLENGE** (a cool micro service site, business start-up project for $50) page 114

- **COURSE-BASED WEBSITE** (a great tool for you and your students) page 109
- **FACEBOOK** (and the second most popular site on the internet is) page 110

Beginning and Ending With a Bang (Art of the Start and Killer Conclusions):

- **BLANK SYLLABUS** (what do you want to do this semester? – ownership, buy-in) page 120
- **POKE FUN AT YOURSELF** (nothing establishes your credentials as one human among others better than an anecdote that is at your own expense) page 122
- **WRITE NAMES** (have students write their names and hometowns on board) page 117
- **TALKING EARLY** (get students talking early—day one) page 126
- **STUDENT NAMES** (nothing sweeter than hearing one's own name) page 117
- **CHITCHAT** (the value of small talk) page 118
- **THE BIG PICTURE** (poster sheets on wall to draw who you are and where you are going) page 123
- **LETTER FROM PRIOR STUDENTS** (give out last semester's letters to new students) page 129
- **54 NUMBERS** (the power of information) page 124

Cheat Sheet

- **TRAFFIC JAM** (group activity to get acquainted with purpose, team building, communication, problem solving) page 123
- **STUDENT HOURS** (post this on your syllabus and door, not "office hours") page 118
- **FIRST DAY/WEEK QUESTIONS** (generate thought and trigger discussion through questions) page 126
- **CAREER CHARADES** (acting out the vocation then discussing salary, education, prognosis, etc.) page 129
- **THEMED POTLUCK** (on last day just before evaluations, or periodic reviews) page 130
- **LETTER TO FUTURE STUDENTS** (great reflection activity with suggestions and information learned) page 128
- **THE 30-SECOND DIFFERENCE** (initial student judgment) page 117
- **JUST A LITTLE EARLY** (what a difference a few minutes makes, start 5 minutes early) page 119
- **THE POWER OF PLAY** (play changes attitudes and behavior, and makes learning last) page 24
- **DESIGN MOTIVATIONAL POSTER** (first day group project perhaps on the virtues of timely homework) page 122
- **FIRST DAY THOUGHTS** (students write one concern and one thing they are excited about) page 126
- **EARLY FIELD TRIP** (get out on day one) page 120
- **THE WRONG WAY** (here's how NOT to present a speech) page 121
- **GET ACQUAINTED** (purposeful introductions relating to the topic) page 122
- **OVERVIEW** (what can I look forward to) page 126

Quick Student Engagement Ideas for Busy Teachers

— **PLAY DOUGH SYMBOLISM** (representation captured from project) page 130

— **POSTER SESSION** (wine and cheese poster sessions to show off student projects) page 130

Enterprising Engagement Model

Movement
"Less Seat Time"

- Motion activation & movement learning

Materials
"Show-N-Tell"

- Sensory engagement & interest impact

Mindfulness
"Flex Your Mind Muscle"

- Mental engagement & thought triggers

Media
"Digital Participation"

- Tradigital content & technology vehicles

NOTES

NOTES

NOTES

NOTES

About the Author

As a recovering lecturer, Russ Johnson makes a living in the classroom and the corporate training room on a variety of topics (change, engagement, creativity, innovation, leadership, inspiration, etc.). His proudly displayed diplomas, albeit a little dusty, come from Brigham Young University (go Cougars!) and American Graduate School of International Management (go T-Birds!). Russ is an inspirational speaker, trainer, educator, performance strategist, and—most important—a life-long student of change and the power that comes from acting on the information we receive.

Founder of: ww.ThePoorTeacher.com and www.Training-For-Change.com. Organizations of all sizes have experienced the passion and energy Russ radiates within moments of his kick-off. He is an in-demand speaker and trainer. *Quick Student Engagement Ideas for Busy Teachers* is Russ's first book. As a speaker/trainer he has introduced these principles to the world of academia and corporate training across the country and Canada and would love to help others be more engaged.

Russ resides in Utah with his most prized possession—his family.

Contact us for your next event (faculty development or professional development).

Let's keep the discussion alive. Please share your successes at capturetraining@gmail.com.

CPSIA information can be obtained
at www.ICGtesting.com
Printed in the USA
FSOW01n2313050717
36034FS